# Wild Garlic

## Culinary Memoirs

*by*

**Peggy Tolleson**

Published by Peggy Tolleson

This book is dedicated to my family,
without whose unstinting help and enthusiastic
encouragement it would not have come to fruition.

A big thank you to all my friends, past and present, who
shared their precious recipes with me.

Wild Garlic

First published in 2007 by Peggy Tolleson

Text and photographs © Peggy Tolleson

ISBN 9780-9557509-0-8

Designed and typeset by Kristi van Riet & Mike Tighe
Watercolours and oil painting of artichoke by Katrina Brashares
Photographs by the author, her family and friends
Printed and bound by Cromwell Press, Trowbridge, UK

# Wild Garlic

# Contents

I am sitting by a stupendous 4000 year-old Menhir in the Cévennes, in Southern France. The sun is shining. My mutt Tess is lying next to me. I am stuffing some wild garlic leaves into my ham sandwich. My mind is wandering. How did I get here? When did I get hooked on cooking and creating new dishes? I decided to write it all down.

*Peggy*

Les Micocouliers, October 2007

# War Years in Switzerland

My grandmother was 62 when I was born (1928) and I don't remember her wearing anything but widow's weeds and heavy skirts almost down to her sturdy lace-up leather boots. Even her aprons were dark grey or black.

She had lovely white hair which she wore in a bun at the back of her head and she looked exactly like a storybook grandmother. When she sat on her chair in front of the Aga stove, a wooden coffee mill between her knees, she could have been posing for Norman Rockwell.

As children we adored watching her wash her hair in front of the big wood burning stove in the living-room. Down would come the tresses, like silver snakes, and her hair would spread out over her shoulders like a mantle. Fascinating for us kids whose mother went to the hairdresser every week and never had a hair out of place.

Looking back after so many years, I wonder what happened between her and my mother. As far back as I can reliably remember, probably to about the age of six or seven, the two never met. My brother and I spent most of our holidays with our grandmother, but she never came to visit us and my mother never went to visit her. It's too late to find out now.

Gais, the town that she lived in, lies in the Canton of Appenzell, which is world-famous for its cheese. But those green pastures, paradise for the picturesque brown cows, need a lot of rain – and they get it! How many times did

we look out of the window forlornly when it rained and rained and rained! My grandmother had a great sense of humour and when the sun finally sent a timid ray across the dining room, she would say: let's tie it down! She would get a piece of thread, pull it through the little holes of the seat of the dining room chairs and symbolically tie the ray of sunshine down…

During the war, there was a shortage of everything. We had ration cards for food and ration cards for textiles. The only thing we had in plentiful supply was grass, mountains and snow. At home we had coal-fired central heating and when there was no more coal, we installed a wood-burning stove in the living room. Schools were privileged and got a certain amount of coal, but from about 1943 on, there simply wasn't any left and, to our great joy, "Choleferie", coal holidays, were proclaimed. Instead of having a measly two weeks at Christmas, we had four, and another five weeks in February.

We kids were immediately sent to our grandmother. At an altitude of 1000m, Gais at that time had snow in the winter. All during the war we had very severe winters. There were

My Grandmother,
Anna Lindenmann,
1866 – 1950

virtually no cars on the road and we had a wonderful time sledding down the main road of the village to the station.

On special occasions we would sled from the Stoss, a famous battle site, down to Altstätten, in the Rhine valley, 600 metres lower, and then take the cog wheel train back home.

Our biggest problem at that time was food. My brother was a teenager, and as such forever hungry. Bread was rationed, like everything else. One day we hatched a scheme. We went to the baker's and bought a large loaf of bread, about 75 centimes at the time. I had previously filled my money purse with lots of small coins: 2 centime pieces, Füferli and Zehnerli (respectively 5 and 10 centime pieces). While I was slowly counting out the change, making a mistake and starting all over again, my brother would take the loaf of bread and open the door, sighing impatiently at my incompetence of counting out the right amount. When I finally got it all, I would hurry out, close the door behind us and race home – the baker had forgotten to ask for the ration card!! A bank robber after a successful heist couldn't have been more proud than the two of us! We pulled this off at three bakeries, but of course couldn't, at least didn't dare, to try it a second time!

My grandmother had a back room where she kept – everything! Every little string, every odd button, empty tea tins, used paper bags, safety pins, empty shoe boxes, old calendars, bits of material, odd balls of wool, old magazines, ancient games, pieces of an old doll house, nothing was ever thrown away: it might come in handy someday, was what she said when we asked her why she hung on to all that stuff. Unfortunately I was living in the States when she died, so was not able to go through her things…

She had an old clock whose heavy brass weights had to be pulled up every morning. That was its winding mechanism. It was a sort of rite of passage to be old enough to pull those always beautifully polished weights up for the first time.

There was only one very large bedroom (what would have been the second bedroom was the above-mentioned "storage room").

I remember three things about that bedroom: first, there was no heat in it. In the winter, my grandmother got out the "Chriesisäckli" (Swiss-German for cherry bags), cloth bags filled with dried cherry pits. Those she kept all day in the "Oferohr", a shelf in the old tiled stove, to warm them, and then placed them in our beds in the evening.

The west wall of the bedroom adjoined the rehearsal room of the *Gaiser Men's Choir* (Gais is the name of the beautiful village that my grandmother lived in). Every Tuesday night they would rehearse all kinds of wonderful old songs. It was heavenly to listen to those voices. I have been told that Eastern Switzerland was, or maybe still is, known for its superb tenors, and I do remember those swelling soaring sounds to this day.

The third thing about that bedroom (even now, when my brother and I get together, we talk about it) was the wallpaper. It depicted wild-looking, fierce, moustachioed hordes of men, curved knives in hand, massacring each other… in vivid colour! Where did that wallpaper come from and why did my grandmother never change it? There are so many things that I will never know the answer to.

My grandmother didn't cook much. She had an Aga stove, but rarely used it. It supplied hot water, but that didn't stop her from putting dark green bottles of water behind the storm windows to be warmed in the sun. She then used the warm water to do the dishes! Most of the cooking was done on two gas rings.

I remember her making the tastiest fried eggs, but that may have been because the free-range eggs were full of flavour in themselves, not because of the way she cooked them.

My grandmother liked to make old-fashioned things like elder blossom lemonade and… Nusstotsch.

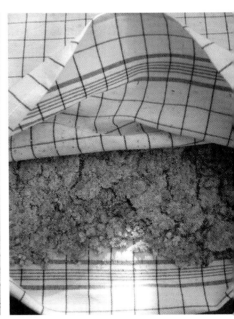

### Nusstotsch

This is a mixture of walnuts, wholemeal bread, sugar and cinnamon and my grandmother made it like this:

She spread a clean kitchen towel on the table, placed on it about 3 cups of day-old, wholemeal bread, broken into small bits, ¾ cup of brown sugar, 2 teaspoons of cinnamon and about 1½ cups of walnut pieces. She then covered this mixture with another clean towel and proceeded to run a rolling pin back and forth over the whole combination until it would almost become a paste. As kids we hardly let her put any away for use in baked apples or pancakes, as it tasted so good.

### My Grandmother's Baked Apples

Use good cooking apples, Bramleys in the UK, russets in the US.

With an apple corer remove the centre of each apple, going in from the top. Make the opening big enough for at least 2 tablespoons of filling, but be careful not to go too far down. You don't want to pierce the bottom; all the good juice would leak out.

Filling: For each medium size apple use 3 tablespoons of the above mentioned Nusstotsch, or mix a tablespoon of brown sugar with a tablespoon of dry bread crumbs and a tablespoon of ground walnuts or hazelnuts. Add a dash of cinnamon and fill the apple cavity with this filling. Top it with a dollop of butter.

Place the apples in an oven proof dish. Stand the dish in a deep baking pan. Fill with water to about half the height of the apples.

Bake for 40 minutes or so in a 350 degrees (175°C) oven. Both types of apples mentioned will fluff up like a soufflé. Serve immediately with whipped cream or vanilla ice cream.

### My Grandmother's Fleischvögel

This is another of my grandmother's special recipes. She made it very rarely, maybe for Easter or a special Sunday, when relatives came for lunch.

Have the butcher cut two thin slices of beef per person. Flatten them with a wooden mallet. Cut sticks of fat bacon, about 1 cm by 1 cm by the width of the slice of beef. Wrap the escalope around the bacon and secure by tying white thread around it. Flour lightly and set aside.
In a bowl soak ½ cup of dried mushrooms in some red wine and warm water.

Heat a tablespoon of corn oil and 2 tablespoons of butter in a thick bottomed casserole. Place the meat in that and brown slowly on all sides. Remove reconstituted mushrooms from the liquid and chop. Add the mushrooms and the strained liquid to the meat. Cover tightly and simmer for about 35 minutes. Remove the threads before serving with mashed potatoes or Türggeribel.

### Türggeribel

This dish is made in the Eastern part of Switzerland, especially in the Rhine valley. The main ingredient is white polenta, which is hard to come by in the rest of Switzerland and even harder here in France.

In the Rheintal Türggeribel is almost as popular as Röschti. If you can get hold of some white cornmeal, here is how you make it:
Boil 1 litre (a generous quart) of milk, add 1 teaspoon of salt and slowly pour 1 lb. (450g) of the polenta meal into the milk, stirring constantly. Reduce the heat and simmer for a few minutes. Cover and let stand for at least 6 hours, best overnight.

When you are ready to cook the Türggeribel, melt 4 tablespoons of clarified butter in a frying pan and add the white polenta to it. With a wooden spoon shift the mixture around constantly; "worry" it until it is brown and crusty throughout.

### Röschti

Everyone has heard about Röschti by now: grated, fried potatoes. You can buy it canned and frozen. The name is related to roast, of course, but it is always fried.
In Switzerland, where Röschti originated, every family has its own favourite Röschti recipe. The only thing every Röschti cook agrees on is that you have to use potatoes that have been boiled at least 24 hours before use. That's the first thing kids learn about Röschti. The second thing is: wash the potato grater with cold water as soon as you are done with it, otherwise you'll need to scrape and brush to get it clean.
You either grate the spuds with a Röschtiraffel, a coarse grater, or slice them.
Any kind of potato can be used, but mealy ones, more suited for mashed potatoes, make mealy Röschti. So it's best to use firm, waxy ones.
For shortening you have the lard brigade, the most traditional of all. Today you hardly find lard in the shops any more, so other fats have taken its place: butter; butter and oil; oil and duck fat or any of these combinations.
During the war, when any kind of fat was extremely rare, you had to stand over the frying pan and stir the potatoes continuously so as to get them cooked through without burning them. And remember, no Teflon…
Some Swiss wouldn't dream of making Röschti

without onions, or without bits of bacon. I like to experiment with different ways of making this traditional Swiss dish and find that there are many variations that show its versatility. I mixed some grated cheddar in it and that tasted very good.

Another time I put some chopped spinach in it with a little grated nutmeg - delicious and pretty. Add a fried egg on top and it's a complete meal.

I next grated some carrots into the cooked potatoes. That was a bit disappointing, but when I added half a cup of fried onions to the carrots, it did the trick and it has become a favourite with my grandchildren.

Another very good mix is chopped red peppers and onions. Chives, parsley, pinto beans, curly cabbage, zucchini, mushrooms… or any of these combinations can all be used for a bit of variety.

My own favourite basic method is as follows:

### Röschti

Peel and grate previously boiled (at least one day before, see page 12) potatoes into a shallow dish. In a heavy skillet melt a mixture of butter, oil and duck fat until almost smoking. Put the potatoes in, turn the heat down two notches, stir with a spatula until the Röschti is warmed through. Add salt and pepper. Now push the potatoes away from the rim of the pan, pat them down a little and let them get brown on the underside. Place a flat dish over the skillet and turn the whole thing upside down, then slide the Röschti back into the skillet and brown the other side. Three or four minutes on each side should be right for a lovely brown colour.

another. In the spring we'd use dandelion greens and poppy leaves, or new spinach and a few crushed juniper berries

## Tante Frieda

One of my grandmother's sisters, as a young lady, wanted to learn French and departed for the Suisse Romande, the French-speaking part of Switzerland. She ended up with a family who lived in Cottens, a village above the Lake of Geneva.

As these things happen, she fell in love with the son of the house and married him.

They bought some land and an old house and set themselves up as farmers. Then disaster struck: the husband was run over by a tractor and lost both legs. Social security didn't exist. They decided to hold on to their farm, but on a smaller scale. They kept a pig and chickens, and my aunt Frieda tended a small vegetable garden. Things were tough though and all the family members did their best to make life tolerable for them.

When I was 12, my father sent me to Tante Frieda and Oncle Victor to improve my French. That is where I first experienced the thrill of living off the land. My aunt took me berrying, mushrooming, gathering wood (which we brought home in an ancient black baby buggy) and picking over wheat fields after the harvest. We brought the awns to the mill and received precious wholemeal flour in return.

I loved the slightly Bohemian life style and I certainly learned to speak French as my uncle did not speak a word of Swiss-German. The

### Plan Wahlen

During the war, when Switzerland was surrounded by the German-Italian Axis, we did not have enough wheat or other cereals, so a very ingenious politician by the name of Wahlen came up with the idea that we should dig up all our lawns and plant potatoes. Which we promptly did and consequently ate a lot of potatoes and made a lot of different potato soups. With a severe shortage of butter and no cream at all, we were hard put to invent all kinds of ways to vary the everyday soup. Here is a recipe. With an addition of bacon cubes or cream, it would provide sturdy, tasty food even today.

### War-time Potato Soup

For every 2 litres of salted water we would use 6 to 8 good sized potatoes. Then we'd add a few carrots and chopped parsley one day, beetroot and chives another, leeks and summer savoury yet only thing I was not terribly keen on was kissing my moustachioed uncle good-night! We ate a lot of freshly dug potatoes from the garden, but my aunt's tour de force was Gschnätzlets, which she made from meat that her slaughtered pig provided.

## Gschnätzlets

Gschnätzlets is almost as ubiquitous in Switzerland as Röschti and is in fact usually served accompanied by the latter.

Most Swiss butchers have a special machine that cuts the meat into small, thin strips. My aunt did all this by hand. First she flattened slices of pork with a wooden mallet and then cut them into diagonal strips. In a heavy skillet she stir-fried the meat for three or four minutes over high heat. With a slotted spoon she removed it from the pan and fried a couple of sliced onions in the remaining fat. Then she added a couple of handfuls of fresh mushrooms, (when I was there, they were fairy ring champignons, mousserons in French), some salt, and lots of chopped parsley and chives, and reintroduced the pork into the mixture. When she decided that the meat was cooked, she stirred in half a cup of the top of the milk (remember, these were war years!) and served the Gschnätzlets with Röschti.

When I make it nowadays, I use soaked, dried porcini or other tasty wild mushrooms, and of course cream. Instead of pork, I usually buy veal or turkey.

*On a Sunday walk with my mother in 1940*

# Pasta Holiday

**I spent the first twenty years of my life in Switzerland. My earliest culinary memory is of Saturday nights: our weekly bath followed by spaghetti with tomato paste and grated cheese. I simply loved the stuff, however un-Italian this way of preparing it may have been.**

Imagine my rapture and excitement when, in 1938, it was decided that we would spend five weeks in Italy, spaghetti land, during the summer holidays!

I was counting the days until we finally boarded a train in Herzogenbuchsee, where we lived, that took us along the Lake of Lucerne, up all those curves to and through the Gotthard tunnel. In Chiasso, at the border between Switzerland and Italy, an Italian custom's official came to collect our passports. A few minutes later he came back, waving them in the air and shaking his head! Was something wrong? I was terrified. Was our trip to the pasta paradise in jeopardy? No, my mother had left the two one hundred Swiss franc notes (yes, enough to cover five weeks in a hotel plus sight-seeing and souvenirs!) in her passport.

What a relief! We arrived in Milan in due time and went to admire the famous dome. My brother and I weren't too impressed or even interested. We found the ice cream vendors with their cries of "Gelati! Gelati!" much more to our taste. For twenty centesimi, which was a tiny amount in Swiss money, we couldn't actually figure out how much, we got a huge ice cream cone. The hardest part was to choose from the dozens of tantalizing flavours!

An auspicious start.

At home everyone had been teasing me and saying I would be getting sick of spaghetti in no time at all. How wrong they were! At our hotel in Grado, a little town on the Adriatic Sea between Venice and Trieste, they served sensational pasta, and I had spaghetti every single day of our stay there.

It was altogether a magical vacation. It was my first time at the seaside and I learned to swim in those shallow, warm waters. We caught crabs, went on pedalos, built sand castles, buried each other in sand and then, tired and happy, I had spaghetti for dinner.

We took steamboat trips to Trieste and some islands whose names I have forgotten; and made friends with some Italian children who introduced us to fishing. Amazingly I avoided getting serious sunburn all summer long. Our mother sat under her umbrella at the beach and made friends with whomever she could, gossiping and exchanging magazines.

I especially remember her talking to a lady in a black bathing suit which covered most of her arms and legs down to her knees. She was telling our mother that she was from Vienna and on her way to the United States. Only much later did it dawn on me that she was Jewish and fleeing from the Nazis.

### Simple Tomato Sauce

Now that I have a vegetable garden I treasure picking the luscious tomatoes. I have found a variety that is perfect for making sauce. When these red wonders are fully ripe the skin comes off easily, without the time-consuming ordeal of dipping them in boiling water first.

Fry 4 onions, finely sliced, in a mixture of olive oil and butter until glassy.

Add 4 cloves of chopped garlic, 2½ lbs. (1.3 kg) of ripe tomatoes, peeled and seeded, and a nice bunch of torn basil.

Cook *slowly* for 40 minutes, stirring frequently, then add 1 tablespoon of brown sugar, 2 teaspoons of salt and cook for another 30 minutes.

Like so many stewed foods, it tastes even better the next day. This freezes very well.

Just before serving, mix half a cup of cream into the sauce. Sprinkle with grated Parmesan. This sauce suits any kind of pasta, but particularly penne.

### Wild Mushroom Bolognaise

Soak 2 oz. (about 50g) of dried wild mushrooms (porcini, Horn of Plenty, or anything you can get) in lukewarm water. Fry 1 lb. (450g) of ground beef slowly in a mixture of vegetable oil and butter. Place in a large casserole. Fry 3 onions, finely sliced, until golden, and add to the meat. Peel and deseed a generous 2 lbs. (1kg) of ripe tomatoes and together with a ½ lb. (225g) can of tomato concentrate combine with the rest of the ingredients, i.e. a bay leaf, 2 cloves of chopped garlic, 2 tablespoons each of dried oregano, dried basil and dried summer savoury, a chicken stock cube and the softened mushrooms in their water. Put everything into the casserole, cover and cook slowly for about 45 minutes.

*Dried wild mushrooms*

### Pasta Sauce with Broccoli and Pesto

Separate 1 lb. (about 450g) of broccoli into little florets and cut the tender parts of the stem into cubes. Discard the tough stalks. Scald for 1 minute in salted water and drain.

In a saucepan heat 2/3 cup of pesto, preferably home-made, see below.

Combine pesto and broccoli and serve on any kind of pasta, accompanied by Parmesan.

### Pesto

In a food processor or blender, put 3 cups of chopped basil, ½ cup of toasted pine nuts (or walnuts), 6 cloves of peeled garlic and 2/3 cup of grated Parmesan and Gruyère. Add ¾ cup of olive oil and ½ tsp. salt. Of course you can adjust all of these quantities to suit your palate.

Make a good quantity and what you don't use right away freeze in an ice cube tray. It will keep its flavour for a couple of months.

### Shrimp Sauce (*opposite*)

Get 2¼ lbs. (1kg) of cooked shrimp. Shell them. Chop and fry the white part of a leek and one finely sliced carrot in a mixture of butter and oil. Add half of the shrimp shells. Stir constantly for 10 minutes. Now add 2 cups (40 cl) of dry white wine and six strands of good quality saffron. Cover and simmer for another 10 minutes. Strain.

You should get about 1½ cups (30 cl) of liquid. Warm the peeled shrimp slowly in this broth. Just before serving adjust the flavour with salt and pepper and add a cup of thick cream.

### Spaghetti con Vongole

This is very time consuming, but oh so good. Vongole are tiny little mussels, called tellines in France. Get 1½ lbs. (700g) for 4 people. Wash under running cold water, then place in a casserole with a tight fitting lid. Add 1 cup of white wine, cover tightly and put on a pre-heated element if you are cooking on an electric stove, otherwise on maximum gas. It will only take about a minute for the little clams to open. As soon as they are all open, take them out with a slotted spoon and put them aside. Strain the remaining liquid through a paper coffee filter or butter muslin.

In a sauce-pan, soak a teaspoon of saffron threads in the sieved liquid. Take the mussels out of their shells and rinse again. Warm the saffron and the mussel liquid very slowly. When the saffron has just about dissolved, add the vongole and half a cup of light cream. Adjust the seasoning and serve on pasta.

### Spaghetti with Egg Yolks and Walnuts

Use 1 ½ egg yolks per person. Whisk them with an egg beater until frothy, season with salt and pepper, add broken walnut pieces and serve uncooked on hot pasta. A bit heavy on the cholesterol, but, using fresh farm eggs this is a treat to enjoy once a year.

### Eggplant Lasagne

Another one of my very favourite Italian dishes is aubergine lasagne, to give it its French name. This is very time consuming, but it freezes well and it's worth making two at a time, one to serve fresh to 6-8 people in the summer, when eggplants are tasty and plentiful, and freezing the other one for the Christmas holidays, when you don't want to spend all your time in the kitchen. Peel 4 medium size eggplant, slice the long way and fry in hot olive oil until light brown. Spread on

paper towels to drain off excessive oil.
In a wide saucepan make a béchamel sauce with 100g (not quite 4 oz) of butter, 1 cup (110g) of flour (I use wholemeal), 2 cups (40 cl) of milk, ¼ tsp. of grated nutmeg and ½ tsp. of salt. When cool, mix with a 500g (1 lb.+) can of tomato concentrate.

Line a rectangular oven-proof dish with a quarter of this sauce. Place a layer of lasagne sheets on top, then a layer of sliced eggplant, followed by one of sliced mozzarella. Repeat until you have used up all the ingredients. Aim to finish with a thin coating of the tomato/béchamel sauce. Sprinkle a handful of grated Parmesan and a dozen leaves of basil over the top. Cover with foil and bake in a medium oven until it smells good. If you are going to freeze it, stop here. To serve, remove the foil, and grill the lasagne for a few minutes.

### Beef and Spinach Lasagne

Fry 500g (1 lb.+) of ground beef until there is no red colour left. With a slotted spoon transfer to a bowl in order to get rid of as much fat as possible.
Boil 500g (1 lb.+) of fresh spinach for 1 minute and drain.
Make béchamel sauce like in the eggplant recipe and add tomato concentrate as above. Proceed as in eggplant lasagne, substituting beef and spinach for the eggplant.

### Sausage and Spinach Lasagne

Use sausage meat instead of ground beef, but fry it until most of the fat has been rendered. Discard that. The method is the same otherwise.

# Sigvard Minck

In 1937 and 1938 my father used to do a lot of mountain climbing with a Swede, Sigvard Minck. He was the most dashing fellow you can imagine. At the ripe old age of 9, I had a huge crush on him.

His mother was Maltese and he had Swedish blue eyes, but very dark hair. He drove a Lancia and he was always terribly kind to me, often driving me to the Konditorei (Swiss pastry shop) and buying me an ice cream cone. Ice cream was a luxury; nobody had a fridge in those days, let alone a freezer! Imagine me sitting in his convertible with my ice cream, while all my friends were looking on! And on some clear summer nights he would drive my father and me far out towards Solothurn where we could have a look at the snow-covered Alps! He actually lived in Tunis, where his father was the Swedish consul. In August of 1939 he and my father had planned to do some serious climbing in the Atlas mountains in Morocco, but the international situation became so alarming that they had to abandon the idea. Sigvard had left a pair of huge car headlights with us.

I have no idea why. I only know that I used to sneak and look at them and pine for my handsome Swede.

When the war broke out we were left with no news from him for a long time. I would look at an atlas and imagine Sigvard living in Tunis, which seemed a very exotic place at that time. Only in 1942 did we get news that in fact he had committed suicide 2 years earlier.

I was unbelievably distressed.

He introduced us landlubbers to gravad lax. Where he managed to get fresh salmon I will never know. He would drive to Bern and come back with the precious stuff and proceed as follows:

**Gravad Lax**

2 slabs of fresh salmon, about ¾ of a pound (330g) each
3½ tablespoons of rock-salt
2½ tablespoons of brown sugar
1 teaspoon of ground black pepper
1 generous cup of chopped, fresh dill

Rinse and towel dry the fish. Rub thoroughly with the salt, sugar and pepper.

Place the first slice skin down into a shallow dish. Cover with the dill. Lay the second fillet on top, skin up. Weigh the fish down with a heavy pot or dish to flatten it. Cover the dish.

Keep in the refrigerator for 48 hours, but take it out twice a day to spread the rendered liquid over the top.

When ready to serve cut into thin, diagonal slices and garnish with dill.

Serve with honey and mustard sauce. Rye bread goes well with this dish.

# Geneva 1947-48

**When I was at law school in Geneva I met my husband-to-be John, who was working on a master's degree in geology at the University of Geneva.**

We happened to both live at the Pension Meuman, but what brought us together was music. I played the piano reasonably well and John had a lovely tenor voice. He had been a successful boy soprano, singing at weddings in the Church of the Heavenly Rest in Manhattan.

Oratorios were his specialty, Handel's Messiah and Haydn's Seasons and Creation being his favourites. We "did" Schumann, Schubert, Brahms and our pièce de résistance was the flower song of Bizet's Carmen, with John hitting that high A to perfection.

Then, together with his fellow Harvard colleague Ted Brown, he decided to found an English language newspaper in Geneva, *The Geneva Transcript*.

It was a weekly that was printed on Thursday, so Wednesday was always chaotic.

At first I just supplied Mettwurst sandwiches to the editorial staff, i.e. John and Ted. Mettwurst is a Swiss smoked meat spread. However I was soon drawn in as a contributor on food and tourism, and especially as proof reader. Ted's girl friend and future wife Maru was also roped in for various chores. What fun we had!

When Mrs. Roosevelt was in Geneva she stopped at our office and gave us a lot of encouragement. It was a wonderful shot in the arm.

At one point there was a printers' strike in Geneva and we had to set the type ourselves, an exhilarating experience. And we ended up being the only newspaper printed that day!

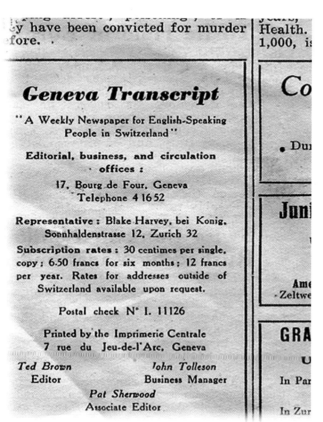

Unfortunately we made no money and the paper eventually folded.

John and I were married at the American Church in Geneva, by Bishop Larned. My father, who was originally bitterly opposed to my marrying an American, relented and gave a splendid reception after the wedding at the Parc des Eaux Vives in Geneva.

## Leaving Europe

In 1948, when we got married, it was quite an event to go to the US. It was therefore with much emotion that I boarded an American Constellation in Croydon, at that time London's airport. Seeing the last of the English countryside beneath me I thought to myself: this is it; my life is now going to be on the other side of the Atlantic, good-bye, Europe! When we landed in Shannon for a stopover, we had dinner at the airport restaurant. At the

table next to us sat an elderly couple, having their soup. The wife looked at her husband and said: Härdöpfusuppe (potato soup) – in the broadest, slowest Bärndütsch (the dialect spoken in the Canton of Bern)! I burst out laughing.

We talked to those two and found out that they had emigrated to the States 40 years earlier and had now gone back to see the old country for a month.

I asked whether they thought about going back to Switzerland for good. They were quite vehement. No, they had been gone too long, but still spoke Schwyzerdütsch with each other. That was not the only surprise our flight with American Airlines had in store for us: because of bad weather the plane was diverted to the US air base in Keflavik, in Iceland, where we were herded into some Quonset huts and served sweet milk coffee for breakfast. We did eventually reach Boston, then took the bus to Denver where John started his job with Sinclair Oil on the 1st of November 1948.

This is a good place to write down a wonderful recipe for traditional post-war potato soup.

### Härdöpfusuppe (opposite)

Slice and sauté a large onion in a mixture of lard and oil. Put into a stew-pot. Repeat same procedure with 2 leeks. Dice 3 carrots, add to the pot.

Peel and dice 8 potatoes (remember, this is not a vegetable soup, but a potato soup), add to the pot.

If you have meat or chicken broth, use that for a liquid, otherwise take water, put in a bone, a chicken stock cube, a bay leaf, a sprig of marjoram, salt and pepper, and cook until done.

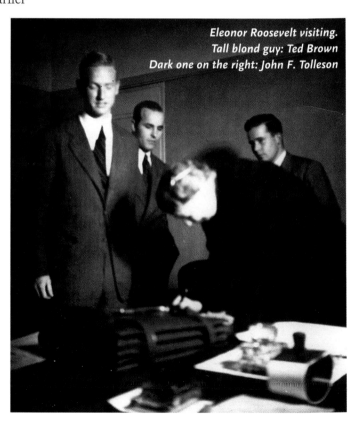

*Eleonor Roosevelt visiting.*
*Tall blond guy: Ted Brown*
*Dark one on the right: John F. Tolleson*

24

# Golden Years

**We started what was to be our very peripatetic married life in Pleasantville, near Golden, just west of Denver, Colorado, in a ramshackle little house with a wood-burning stove and a well.**

My father, having no idea how primitive our abode was, had some Biedermeier furniture dating from about 1815, and Persian carpets sent over from Switzerland. So there we were, with a lovely period chest of drawers, a walnut wood desk, a Tabriz carpet, a stately Neuchâtel clock and a couple each of mugs, plates, knives and forks from Woolworth's – plus a piano, bought for $25, stripped down and painted pink!

The rent for this house in Golden was $45 a month. That was in 1949.

Pleasantville was a very euphemistic name: in fact we lived out on the prairie. Our mailbox was about 1 mile down the road.

Our nearest neighbours had an equally ramshackle house, but it was rather more crowded. Helen and Malcolm Cash had four young children, two cats and two dogs. We promptly acquired two of their kittens, Plain Jane, a beautiful all grey hussy, and Dotty, the most wonderful cat it has been my privilege to give a home to.

The two of them gave us great pleasure over the next seven years!

Helen Cash was a great help to me. Here I was, a newly married Swiss girl of 20 in a foreign country; nearest family, in-laws at that, were 3000 km away, I had no friends, no driver's license, an American husband at work all day, sometimes well-sitting, i.e. supervising the drilling of an oil well, for several days in a row. So naturally my comfort lay in the affection of our dog, an abandoned Great Dane, and cats – and Helen. Helen introduced me to corn on the cob and sweet potatoes as well as avocados, which she used in fruit salad. She taught me how to make American biscuits, told me where to get

*Our house and the Nash. January 1949*

peaches for two Dollars a bushel and gave me a recipe for spiced peaches.

She also revealed the efficiency of the washing machine to me. I had never seen one before.

### Spiced Peaches

Make a syrup with 3½ cups (500g) of light brown sugar, 2 cups (40 cl) of cider vinegar, ½ cup (10 cl) of water. Add one stick of cinnamon, 1 teaspoon of cloves and 1 teaspoon of mustard powder.
Peel about 4 lbs.( 1¾ kg) of firm peaches. Place into the syrup and boil slowly for 4 minutes.
Put into sterilized Mason jars and seal.

It was Helen also who showed me how to use a whole raw red cabbage as a base, garnish it with cubes of cheese and ham, radishes, green and black and olives, bits of red pepper, all skewered on toothpicks and stuck into the cabbage to make it look like a colourful porcupine. This she served with drinks. I used that idea for cocktail parties many a time all over the world much later. When we lived in London, I used Derby Sage, a green cheese, and Windsor Red, as its name implies, a reddish one, to great effect. Sadly, when we moved up to the hills, the Cash family moved to the Midwest and we lost touch with them.

## Afton and Lake Alice

We were unbelievably lucky in the places where the oil company sent John to do field work: Walden, Colorado; Afton, on the border of Wyoming and Utah; Jackson Hole, and the Tetons.

*Helen Cash and Honey*

We started out in Afton.

Because the terrain where we had to do mapping was only accessible by horse, the Sinclair Petroleum Company, our employer, hired a wrangler and six horses, four to ride on (there was a second geologist) and two to carry the equipment and food.

The wrangler, Gene, was in charge of the tent, the horses and the food. This was quite a handful, but he managed everything with panache.

Our first camping site was on the shores of Lake Alice. Remember, this was in 1949 before tourists discovered that area and Jackson Hole. Not only was it breathtakingly beautiful and quiet, but the lake itself also provided us with more trout than we could ever eat.

The very first time in my life that I held a fishing rod in my hand, I caught a trout within one minute. "Reel it in, reel it in!" John shouted, but I had no idea what that meant. I held the rod up in the air and walked backwards away from the lake, until the men took control. How they laughed at me….

Gene's breakfasts were a revelation. Even with

all of the tent gear, cooking utensils, sleeping bags and mapping paraphernalia he had to bring, he didn't neglect food. He actually bought and mixed white, wholemeal and rye flour before we left Afton, in order to make delicious pancakes. And of course he brought maple syrup along. The only thing that put me off slightly was the sight of bacon, eggs and pancakes on his plate, <u>all</u> soaked in syrup. De gustibus… and as he pointed out, it all ended up in the same place.

I later recreated a version of those pancakes, but none of them ever tasted as good as Gene's, cooked over the camp fire.

### Yeast Pancakes

1 cup of white flour (110g)
1 cup of whole wheat flour (110g)
½ cup (55g) each of buckwheat flour and rye flour
Optional: wheat germ, wheat bran, oat germ, oat bran
1½ (30 cl) cups of milk
1 egg
¾ tsp. salt
½ ounce (about 15g) of fresh yeast
or ½ package of dry yeast
Water

   If possible, prepare the mixture the night before, stirring all the ingredients together and leave in the fridge overnight. In the morning add water to the desired consistency. Otherwise, leave the dough at room temperature until you see a few bubbles forming. Again, if it is too dense, add some cold water.

To top it all off, we finished our summer in Jackson Hole, camping beside a creek which was full of water cress, and directly in front of the Grand Tetons. It was magical.

I had my second fishing experience about two years later. Chrish, our oldest, was five or six months old. My husband wanted to go fishing in one of the creeks about an hour from where we lived. I put the baby in a basket, collected a couple of books and tagged along.

John put on his hip boots and went off.

A good hour later I was getting a bit restive; no John, no cries of WOW, no swearing, nothing. Suddenly I heard some splashing. And there, right next to me, I saw a trout, thrashing to get out of a little pool where it had gotten caught. My ur-hunting instincts took over. I dropped the book and went after the poor fish and managed to catch it with my bare hands, but I had no idea what to do with it, so I screamed my head off.

John came rushing from wherever he had been, thinking I was either being aggressed or the baby had fallen into the creek. As he liked to tell the story later, he saw me clutching the trout so hard, its eyes were bulging! He took it from me and gave it the coup de grâce. I never tried fishing again and never even held a dead trout in my hand again.

When Chrish was seven months old, we decided to go back east and show her off. We had a rather elderly Nash automobile, but it got us all the way to Boston.

My father-in-law and I didn't really hit it off. He could never understand why his only son had to get himself a foreign wife. And I

was not overly fond of his dachshunds, who barked non-stop. He did however adore his granddaughter and that sort of brought us together.

The house he owned and lived in was a wonderful old New England clapboard cottage, the Deacon Thayer House in Braintree, Massachusetts.

He served us some delicious food. He was originally from South Carolina (his grandfather on his mother's side had founded the little town of Gaffney, S.C.) and his cooking was inspired by the South. He made the best Southern Fried chicken.

For breakfast he sometimes made "bapple":

### Bapple

Peel, core and slice 3 or 4 cooking apples. Sprinkle them with sugar and cinnamon and bake them until almost done. Place rashers of bacon over the top and grill the whole thing until the bacon starts to brown.

I was originally very wary of bacon and apples (hence bapple), but once I tried it I couldn't get enough of it, and it became a staple in our family.

## Kushary

This recipe came to me through quite an extraordinary person whom I met by an extraordinary coincidence.

We were doing geological field work in Western Colorado in 1949 and the nearest post office was in Craig, Colorado.

When I went to mail a letter to my parents in Switzerland, the clerk looked at me and said, "To Switzerland? Are you Swiss? "

I said yes, whereupon he told me that his neighbours were Swiss and I should meet them. And we did!

Mimi and Carl were quite unusual in many ways. She was French-speaking and he was Swiss-German-speaking, but because they couldn't speak each other's languages, their conversations took place in very heavily accented English.

Mimi had been a governess in Egypt for many years and was now giving piano lessons in Craig. Carl had worked his way around the world as a sailor. They met in Alexandria and decided to get together. How they wound up in Craig, I don't remember. Carl was a road worker, but his passion was making his own beer and hunting and fishing.

One day they took us up to their little cabin in the woods and proceeded to take out some trout from the creek nearby (you couldn't call it fishing. All you had to do was put the rod in and pull it out again - et voilà, a trout!) When I asked her if the fishing season was open, Mimi laughed and said, "Oh, no. I just open it a little bit and close it again behind me!"

I remember a slightly adapted Egyptian Kushary which she used to serve.

### Kushary

Soak 1 cup each of brown rice, green lentils and spelt overnight or in the morning for use in the evening.

When you are ready to cook, add a few unpeeled cloves of garlic, a bay leaf and a chicken stock

cube and simmer until just done. Don't overcook. Adjust the seasoning. Serve with yoghurt.

**For a deluxe edition of Kushary (***above***):**
Roast, skin and deseed two red peppers. Slice and fry one aubergine. Slice one green and one yellow zucchini and stir-fry. Separately, slice and fry two onions until they turn almost black.

Proceed like for simple Kushary and serve the vegetables on the side.

Top the mixture with the crispy fried black onions. In Egypt, they also serve it with plenty of hot sauce sprinkled on top.

So simple, so healthy and so delicious!

PS: a year later I happened to be in Craig again, three months pregnant, and needed to get a maternity dress. I went to J.C. Penney's and asked a young man there, "Do you have maternity wear?" He replied, "Ladies'?"
You can imagine how he blushed when he realized what he'd just said!

# Back to Europe

When, in 1955, John was offered a job as manager of an oil and gas exploration company in Switzerland, we jumped at it. We found a most wonderful family house to rent in Küsnacht, on the Lake of Zürich.

In order to furnish it we were paid three months in advance. But not until well into the second month did I realize that we wouldn't get paid for four months, so we had to put the brakes on expenditures. I gave birth to our third daughter Andrea a month after arriving back in Europe, on the 5th of May, 1955, i.e. 5/5/55!

## Siponto

In the summer of 1956, our theater of operations included Italy, and when John spent most of his time in Foggia, near the "spur" of the peninsula of southern Italy, we decided to move to the region for a couple of months. I bundled our three girls, the housekeeper, Frau Saitz, and the dog into our Opel station wagon and drove down to southern Italy. We found a villa for rent in Siponto, a town that had been settled by the ancient Greeks in the first century B.C. The house was situated a couple of hundred yards from the beach, on the Gulf of Manfredonia. It was surrounded by a high wall the top of which was covered with glass shards, in order to keep out burglars. To no avail.

Late one night Madie, our dog, began to growl fiercely. I told her to be quiet and went back to sleep. The next morning we found that some burglars had stolen most of our clothes and all of our shoes…

On the culinary front, we bought kilos of wild strawberries from the hills between Foggia and Naples. I also ate the best risotto in my life in a little restaurant in Manfredonia, as well as the best ever pizza, baked in literally a hole in the wall, in a simple workman's pizzeria in Foggia. We grilled eels on the beach and our Italian housekeeper showed us how to make scrumptious…

### Calamari Brochettes

I use the small calamari that have a little crown on the top, called supions here. Alternate red and green pepper strips, slices of onion, squares of bacon and supions, brush with olive oil and grill 4-6 minutes on each side.

## Pastry Thieves

We spent the winter months in Davos, Switzerland, where I decided to put my reasonably good skiing to some use and become a ski instructor.

The first two years we had to help out in the children's classes and it involved mainly blowing snotty noses, comforting, encouraging and making sure we finished the lesson with the same amount of kids as when we began. Not too much actual teaching of snow-plows!

Twice a week we had "instructors' training". This was interesting, but it was sometimes so cold I was afraid my face would get frost-bitten. I remember one night, when it was minus 24 centigrade and we were being taught to teach snow-plows, I almost gave up. But somehow I persevered and after two years and an intensive three week final course, I proudly wore the badge of a professional Swiss ski instructor.

My Danish friend Anna and her Swiss husband Johnny were also ski instructors. We often went schussing down the slopes together when ski school was over and managed to get absolutely famished.

One afternoon we were all planning to have dinner together, and after doing the final ski run, Anna and I went to the Konditorei (pastry shop) Café Weber to buy dessert, fourteen

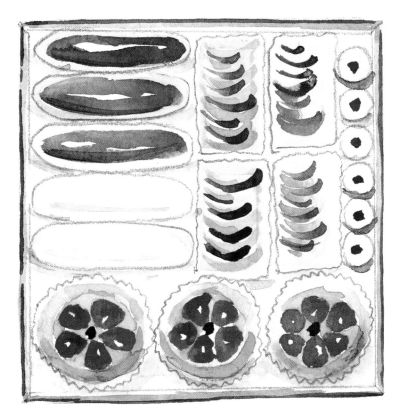

pastries, two for each of us. When we got back to the car we were so hungry we decided to eat one pastry each, so that Anna and I would then only have one each for our dessert. But once we started, we couldn't stop. First we reasoned that one for everybody would be enough, then we decided that we would have both of ours now instead of for dessert - and we finally ended up eating all fourteen pastries!

We felt wonderfully satisfied, albeit rather ashamed…

And that was when another one of my larder and freezer emergency supply recipes came in handy:

### Mock Pavlova

We took blackberries, raspberries, strawberries and black currants from the freezer and made compote with them. In the larder we got some meringues and some long life cream. So into individual dessert bowls we crumbled a meringue shell, spooned some berry compote over it and topped it with the cream.

We had a delicious and very popular dessert in a jiffy and didn't tell anybody about our greedy deed until later!

Needless to say, this is a godsend of a recipe when you have to make a dessert for unexpected guests.

For a different version, caramelize one pound of frozen raspberries in half a cup (110g) of sugar and the juice of half a lemon. Add ½ a cup (10 cl) of white rum and the juice of an orange. Pour over crumbled meringues and top with whipped cream.

Here is Anna's delicious chocolate cake recipe

### Anna's Chocolate Cake

¼ lb. (110g) each of sugar, cooking chocolate and butter
2 scant oz. (50g) flour
3 eggs
Separate the egg yolks from the whites. Melt the butter and chocolate in a double boiler. Add the sugar, egg yolks, flour and finally the beaten egg whites.

Pour into a prepared cake pan and bake at low temperature 160F (320°C), for 30 or 40 minutes. Double the quantity for a more substantial cake.

# Denmark Days

In the summer of 1957 I left my three daughters in the excellent care of Frau Saitz, our housekeeper and nanny, and went with my Danish friend Anna to visit her folks in Denmark.

I shudder when I think that without giving it a second thought we pulled the station wagon off the Autobahn in Germany and spent the night in it on the side of the road. It simply didn't occur to us that it might be dangerous for two girls in their twenties to leave themselves vulnerable to potential robbers, or worse. Of course we were perfectly fine.

That night we took the ferry from Grossenbrode to Gedser, arriving there at about 4 am and again pulled the car into a meadow and slept in it until 7am.

Visiting Denmark was a strange experience for me, like a déjà-vu.

Everything seemed so familiar - and so good. The landscape, the lovely old houses, the food, all those hollyhocks, the people, it was a true revelation. The most ordinary mundane things were made in such good taste.

I bought a large, black enamel salad bowl and a teak wood pepper mill with matching salt shaker at the Permanente, a wonderful department store in Copenhagen. I have them to this day, having moved them from Switzerland, to France, to Tunisia, to England, to the States and back to Europe again.

This is not the place to go into a description of the castles, or the Tivoli, the Den Gamle By in Aarhus, or even the Louisiana museum. But please look them up on the internet – they are spectacular!

We went swimming in the sea at 10 pm and it was still light. And everyone was always inviting us for coffee and cake… It was an altogether perfect trip.

Among the many things that I ate in Denmark for the first time is *rød kål*, red cabbage, best served with pork roast

**Danish Red Cabbage**
Split a 2 kg (4 ½ lbs.) red cabbage into quarters. Remove the hard white root in the middle and all the leaves until you get to the really shiny part of the cabbage and shred that. Melt 2 tablespoons of duck fat (which you have kept from the last time you fried up a duck magret) or lard in a heavy casserole,

add half of the finely shredded red cabbage and stir to coat it all over. Let the cabbage cook for a couple of minutes, then add the other half.

Chop one medium sized apple into the cabbage, add ¹/3 cup of red currant jelly, 4 tablespoons of cider vinegar. Cook, covered, over slow heat until done. Adjust seasoning.

Another very Danish dish is leverpostej, pork liver pâté:

### Leverpostej

Blend ½ lb. (220g) fresh pork's liver with ¼ lb. (110g) of white, smoked bacon, one medium sized onion, 4 tablespoons of whole-wheat flour, 1 cup (20 cl) of milk, half a raw, grated potato, ½ teaspoon of nutmeg, 1 teaspoon of black pepper and ½ teaspoon of salt until you have a coarse purée. Pour into a rectangular cake pan and place into a larger baking dish that you have filled with water (bain-marie). Bake in a slow oven until a toothpick stuck in it comes out clean.

Delicious when served warm, with boiled potatoes, or of course as a cold pâté. Or, with:

### Danish Bread

Mix together 2.2 lbs. (1kg) of different flours (whole wheat, rye, buck wheat, fine polenta, a bit of oat germ), add 2 teaspoons each of sugar and salt, 1 tablespoon of oil, 1 oz. (30g) of yeast, 5 cups (1 litre) of water and pour into 2 oiled and floured bread pans. Place in a cold oven and bake at 360F (185°C) for about one hour.

Eight years later I made my second visit to Denmark. We had become good friends with

Ilia and Poul, and Frants and Elisabeth, two Danish couples whom we had met skiing in Davos, so we decided to visit them. We arrived on my birthday, and to my surprise there were flags hanging from every building. Poul, ever the jokester, said, "Yeah, you can imagine how much that cost me!"

It turned out to be Danish National Day! In the late afternoon we went to the Tivoli, Copenhagen's famous amusement park. As we made our way to the entrance, a band of musicians in colourful uniforms marched up, right in front of us! Poul rolled his eyes and said, "Imagine how much *that* cost me!" All this set the tone for a few days of wonderful fun.

Poul's wife Ilia was half Mexican. She liked to use Danish staples and add Mexican flavours to them. In this instance it was shrimp.

This is how she made the most superb shrimp cocktail:

### Ilia's Shrimp Cocktail

Make a sauce with mayonnaise (I have found that ready made mayonnaise works very well), ketchup, lemon juice, Harissa or Tabasco.
Add cooked shrimp, a cubed, tart apple, some finely sliced raw celery and avocado, and serve on lettuce leaves.

As a follow-up to the story I must relate what happened when Ilia and Poul came to visit us in England. We went to the White City Stadium in London to attend an equestrian event and got there very late due to horrendous traffic. As we walked through the entrance, we were suddenly shoved against a roped-off area by policemen. Reason? The Queen was arriving! And there she was, walking past us within touching distance.

Of course I turned to Poul and said, "How much do you think that cost me?"

The next evening we were having a nightcap in the garden at about midnight, when, looking up in the sky, we saw a satellite cruising on its orbit. This was in 1964, so it was a very new sight. Guess what I said to Poul…

# Sidi Bou Said

We lived in Tunisia, in Sidi Bou Said, in 1957 and 1958. This was before tourism took hold in Tunisia. Whenever we visited some magnificent Roman ruins, we had them completely to ourselves.

Dougga, probably the most beautiful of them all, was deserted. We had picnics there with the kids running around the forum, picking up small Roman mosaic pieces and creating their own mosaics with them.

The beaches were pristine. There was one called Monkey Beach (Baie des Singes), where we used to dig up little mussels to eat for dinner. My oldest daughter learned to read and write with the help of big letters carved in the golden sand there.

The house we lived in had been built by a Tunisian architect living in Sweden. He combined the classical Arab style with modern Swedish materials to create a simply breath-taking edifice. It was situated on a promontory overlooking the bay of Tunis. It had a sunken terrace amid marble walls where even on the hottest summer days we were able to eat in comfort. The children's bedroom had huge picture windows on three sides, making it feel like a glass ship on the Mediterranean.

Our cook's name was Fatma, of course. During most of the time that she worked for us she was pregnant and refused to drink water during Ramadan, the Muslim fast, and she would frequently faint and have to be carried home. But oh, the couscous she made!

I would drive her husband Ahmed to do the shopping at the truly wonderful open market in Tunis.

It was a picture book place.

All the colourful vegetables were artfully displayed, the fruit heaped high, the vast array of fish shimmering in the veiled light, sides of lamb and skinny chickens hanging on hooks, and flowers, flowers everywhere. While Ahmed haggled and bought lamb and vegetables, I'd wander through the market and fill my arms with flowers.

*Our terrace in Sidi Bou Said*

## Couscous

Fatma's couscous was so divine, and my few attempts at imitating it when living in Europe again, so pathetic that I now make only a much abbreviated practical, vegetarian version. For the real thing go to the recipe on page 100.

### Quick Couscous

During the summer I roast the following in a slow oven: aubergines, red and green peppers, lots of onions, yellow and green zucchini, a clove of garlic or two, sprinkled with a generous amount of olive oil. I don't put any tomatoes in it. I freeze this in plastic containers.

I also soak and then boil 2 lbs. (900g) of organic chickpeas with a head of unpeeled garlic and 1 teaspoon of salt until done, but not mushy. I make portions of 1-2 cups and freeze those. In the winter I cut up and boil a large bunch (about 2 lbs. or 900g) of cardoons, divide them into portions and freeze them.

I heat some thin canned tomato purée, add couscous spice and harissa, mix with the roast vegetables, add a portion each of chickpeas and cardoons, and serve on instant whole wheat couscous grain. It is ready in a jiffy and so good. If you don't want to go vegetarian, just add bits of cooked mutton or chicken.

I had my fourth child, John Jr., in Tunisia. It was fortunate that 1958 was the year of the A-line, narrow top, wide skirt dress. A very good friend of ours, Germaine Bennatar, was a high calibre couturière. She had worked for Dior in Paris before settling in Tunis, and became the legal representative for the house of Dior there. This enabled her to get patterns and fabrics from the high priestess of chic. Germaine made me the most exquisite dress in chalk grey silk with black polka dots, perfect as a maternity dress.

She was also a fine cook and she impressed me with her painstaking way of preparing things. For drying salad she used a thin piece of muslin and dabbed each leaf of lettuce with it. No salad spinner for her.

She made a side dish of tomatoes and red peppers which she called méchouia, meaning basically anything roasted. When I tried to recreate it, I was having a lot of trouble; it just never seemed to taste like anything resembling her creation.

What I eventually figured out (I wasn't able to ask her as she had died before I got around to making it) was that you have to "égoutter", drain, the chopped tomatoes and peppers in order to intensify the flavour. Here is how I make it now:

### Méchouia

Skin, deseed and chop 2 large, very ripe tomatoes. Grill, skin, deseed and chop 2 fleshy red peppers.

Sprinkle with rock salt and let them rest until cold. Put them in a colander and let all the juices run out, even squeezing them a little bit.

Place in a pretty dish and pour 1/3 cup of very good olive oil over them.
For best taste, serve the following day.

I have tried adding garlic or basil or black pepper, but find the very plain recipe best.

Every once in a while I also managed to talk her into serving lab-labi. This dish is the Tunisian working man's meal and her cook was loath to make it as she thought that it wasn't fit to be set in front of Madame's guests.
How wrong she was!
It is a feast for the eyes and the palate.

**Lab-labi** (*above*)
For 4-6 people soak 1 lb. (450g) of good quality, if possible organic, chickpeas overnight.
The next day boil them with a head of unpeeled garlic and a teaspoon of salt or a chicken stock cube until done, but not mushy. Be sure to keep them in their liquid.
While they are cooking, arrange individual

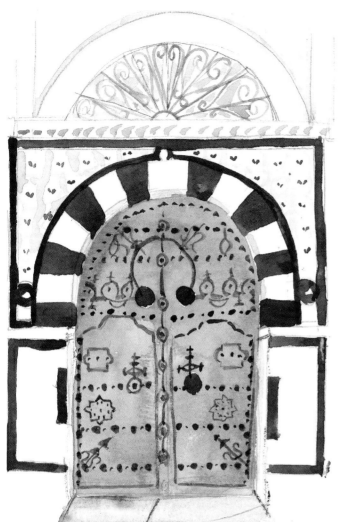

## Shorba

Shorba just means "soup" in Arabic, but in our family it is a specific chicken soup. It's the equivalent of the Jewish chicken noodle soup, with the noodles replaced by bulgur and featuring a typically Arab touch, fresh mint. It has that same comfort-food feeling about it. To have it really perfect you must allow a lot of time. But it freezes beautifully, (I found a container of it in the bottom of the freezer that was dated from 2 years ago. I was a bit reluctant to eat it, but it was fine!) So make plenty! You will be happy to heat some up on a cold winter's day.

### Shorba

Use a large stew pot and place 1 or 2 hens in it. Cover with cold water, add 3 chicken stock cubes, four substantial sprigs of mint and let it come to the boil. Simmer until the flesh comes off the bones. Lift the chicken carefully into a colander which you have placed over a bowl.

Let cool, then skin and de-bone. I like to degrease the broth, so I let it cool off in the fridge overnight. The next day I skim off the fat. Now slice thinly and fry until pale golden 3 medium sized onions. Chop 4 large branches of celery. Place onions and celery into the broth, add 1½ cups of coarse bulgur (cracked wheat), cook until the celery is done; add the chicken, cut into bite-sized pieces. Freeze, or serve with a teaspoon of fresh mint in each bowl.

bowls of croûtons, canned tuna fish, Tunisian harissa, capers, lemon wedges and powdered oriental cumin on the dining table, next to a little jug of extra virgin olive oil. Bring the chickpeas to the table hot in their broth.

Now for each serving crumble a few croûtons in a soup bowl, add some tuna, capers, cumin, harissa, lemon juice and olive oil. Pour the chickpeas over the top, mix to your liking – bon appétit!

# Paris in the Sixties

We had a full time nanny, plus a daily "femme de ménage", as well as Félicité, who came twice a week to iron and mend. And still I was always on the go. The older two children had to be driven to the École Active Bilingue, near the Eiffel Tower, then be picked up and brought to ballet and piano lessons or birthday parties.

There were a lot of VIPs working with John who managed to route themselves through Paris, so I had to arrange cocktail parties and dinners or, what became a bane, take them out to the Folies Bergères and the Paris Lido. I hasten to add that they both offer a splendid spectacle, but not as a steady diet!

The nicest part of having so many visiting big shots coming to Paris was the dining out. Only the best restaurants featured: La Tour Blanche, Maxim's, Le Coq Hardi with its gorgeous display of hydrangeas, the "in" Russian restaurant YAR, just to mention a few. My favourite was Marius et Janette. They had the most delicious seafood, but I notice in the Michelin Guide that they have now lost their 3 star rating.

Living in Paris in the early sixties with four children was not easy. For staples like pasteurized milk and cornflakes or Rice Krispies I had to drive right across Paris to the embassy commissary which catered to American tastes.

I remember well an occasion when the waiter, before putting the food on John's plate, caught the odour of the dish in his cupped hand and wafted it in front of John's nose, much to his delight and subsequent imitations at gatherings.

To get away from all that socializing we rented a "chasse", a hunting lodge, in a forest that included a license for hunting. Together with our friends the Foxes and the Mayers, we would bundle the kids into the car and join the weekend exodus towards the Loire. The game was not plentiful, but it was a lovely place for walks and for wild mushrooms, which at that time started to become our passion.

On one occasion our dear friend Nanny Gasser came with us and gathered poisonous looking purple mushrooms, assuring us that they were perfectly fine. That night we cooked them up. My husband, ever ready for a bit of fun, lit black candles on the table and put on Chopin's Funeral March! Needless to say, we had a most delicious mushroom dinner and no one got sick!

Another way to take some of the stress off my

A day's collection from the woods including amethyst deceivers and a cèpe.

shoulders was to go down to the Germaine Monteil salon at the bottom of the Champs Elysées for a massage. Madame Hélène, who was Vietnamese, gave very good body massages in the basement of the establishment.

She was a fountain of wisdom. More than forty years ago she warned me not to use commercial body lotion. "You never know what all they put in it", she used to say. I presume that her employer upstairs had no idea that there was sabotage going on in the basement. She advised me to mix my favourite cologne with olive oil and apply it with a loofah, a horse hair glove, rubbing especially hard where the dreaded cellulite was most prevalent, on the thighs. I do it to this day.

She would finish off the massage with a short interlude in what I called the fire engine room: a long hall where I held on to a railing and she ran a fire hose over my body, first warm, warmer, and then *cold*… It felt wonderful, and I still do the cold shower after a nice warm bath, an excellent tonic and pick-me-up. Afterwards I would emerge onto the bustling Champs Elysées in a state of euphoria that lasted all day. One day I walked up that famous avenue and stopped at the Prisunic, a 5 and 10 cent store, but which sported some amazingly chic clothes every so often. I spotted a knitted cotton two-piece suit for ninety-nine francs ($18 at the time!). I bought a white one, went home to try it on and liked it so much that I returned forthwith and bought a beige one! Those suits lasted many years and stood me in good stead. Madame Hélène was always full of practical advice on health, food, life in France…

"Never sit down to put on your socks or panty hose", she would say. "Stand on one leg and practice keeping your balance". It's good advice, not so easy to follow at my age.

She thought the best thing the French did food-wise was to eat so much vegetable soup. Not complicated, just basic carrot, leek, turnip and potato combinations. And it is true that wherever I was able to observe a French family, the children had vegetable soup every night, followed by a bit of cheese or a slice of ham and a chunk of baguette. No hot dogs, no hamburgers, no pizza, no chicken nuggets, no coke. I don't remember ever seeing any over-weight French children at that time.

We talked a lot about cooking and it was she who gave me the recipe for the pork dish I call:

### Saigon Pork

Cut 2 pork fillets into slices the long way. With a sharp knife cut the slices into strips, the strips diagonally into small bits, like for stir frying. Place into a dish.

Shred a whole onion and a whole pear over the meat; add a handful of chopped dried cherries, 2 tablespoons of finely chopped fresh ginger and 1/3 a cup of soy sauce.

Stir, cover with saran wrap and marinate for at least two hours.

Heat 2 tablespoons of good cooking oil (corn oil or peanut oil) in a skillet, pour the meat mixture into it and cook, stirring continuously for ten minutes, then add 1½ cups (30 cl) of red wine.

Simmer for another 10 minutes and serve on Basmati rice. Sprinkle with grilled black sesame seeds.

# England

When we were transferred to England I wasn't all that happy about it; I had gotten used to living in Paris and had made lots of friends there.

We were very lucky to find a totally different, but equally comfortable house in London. It was a typical red brick structure, perfect family house, with six bedrooms, a cosy breakfast room, a nice living room and dining room and a garden. It was situated in St. John's Wood, within easy walking distance of schools, the underground, a bus stop, a post office, Panzer's Delicatessen and Mountjoy, the well-known butcher's. And the butcher it was who introduced us to English lamb. What a revelation!

We ate chops and rolled shoulders and roasted ribs and the best of all: leg of lamb, cut in the butterfly style, i.e., you cut the joint apart at the short end of the leg and spread it in such a fashion that it looks like a giant butterfly. This we would marinate for several hours in rosemary, garlic and olive oil, then barbecue.

Just as we had settled in London, we were transferred to Milan, Italy. I wasn't prepared to expose the children to one more language. They had good German and French, and Italian I thought was going to be too much.

We decided to hire a tutor for them who would keep up the German and French. So off we went, house-hunting around Milan. We found an old, romantic place north of the city, near a lake; we sent our yellow Labrador, Biscuit, to friends, the Foxes, in Paris; and moved into the Hilton for a few days… and were then promptly re-transferred to London! In the meantime the house in St. John's Wood had been rented to someone else, the dog would have to go into quarantine for six months, and the tutor became redundant… oh boy!

We were unable to find any suitable housing in London and decided to

live in the countryside. Some friends of friends owned a cottage in Warfield near Bracknell in Berkshire. They themselves were living abroad and agreed to let us rent the place. It was a lovely, typically English dwelling, with a thatched roof, and it went by the name of Cuckoo Cottage.

After one year, when the owners returned from overseas, we moved back to London, smack into the centre, on Welbeck Street, within walking distance of Oxford Street, the Wigmore Hall and the Wallace Collection. No garden, and a terrace that was so covered in soot that we had to wipe the cat's paws when he came in from "doing" the roofs and terraces. To compensate for the lack of green space and good air, we bought a camper van (*above*). Every weekend we would join the throngs and go out into the country. Since our whole family has a passion for wild mushrooms, July, August, September and October would find us looking for spots where there was a likely mushroom bounty. We took eggs

and bacon with us, for a sturdy breakfast, but other than that it was onions, garlic, cream and instant mashed potatoes, the sine qua non for a wonderful mushroom feast.

We weren't always successful, but one day we drove out to Norfolk, near Brandon, and happened on a good spot where we found suillus granulatus, a delicious mushroom, very popular in North Africa. After a tasty dinner, my oldest daughter Chrish and I washed the dishes, while our respective intrepid husbands went out looking for mushrooms *with a flashlight!*

Imagine our surprise when they came bouncing back with bags full of xerocomus badius, the Bay Boletus! Beautiful, fresh specimens. We could hardly wait to go out in the morning and pick more of these lovely mushrooms.

In all, we easily gathered 15 pounds (± 6 kg). We dried most of them for use in the non-mushroom-growing months.

Our interest in mushrooms even extended to design. Katrin, who was attending the Inchbald School of Design, came up with the idea of creating a free-standing mushroom-shaped dining table for the kitchen. She incorporated an electrical hob where the stem was, and covered the "mushroom hat" with cork tiles (*left*). It seated up to eight people, and she won first prize in design for it.

John loved cooking

when there was an audience and he used to make the most delicious goulash, with us sitting around the mushroom table, keeping him company. When John made goulash, it wasn't just a matter of putting ingredients in a pan and cooking them. It was a dramatic, artistic and philosophical culinary event. The only meat that would do, was fillet of the neck of lamb and it had to come from Allen's the butcher on Mount Street. The paprika had to be ultra-fresh, the carrots cut just so. He selected the dried mushrooms himself for crunchiness, size and colour. The onions had to be cut in half, then sliced, NOT chopped. The kitchen was turned into a stage. Two cutting boards, two frying pans, a big iron casserole, spices lined up, various utensils at the ready. First he rid the meat of all the fat and little veins and cut it into bite-sized chunks. These he fried until brown, sprinkled paprika over them, stirred them a couple of times and put them into a large, heavy casserole. He then poured ½ a glass of red wine into the frying pan, scraped it well and poured that over the meat. In another frying pan (we were there to clean up afterwards!) he sautéed the sliced onions very slowly for about 20 or 25 minutes, stirring occasionally. All this was of course accompanied by some loud Verdi or Puccini, with John humming or singing along. Onions done to his satisfaction, they joined the meat.

Then it was the turn of the carrots. He peeled them and cut them into 1¼ inch (± 3 cm) length pieces. Those were sliced into four at a bias and added to the casserole.

Then came: a bay leaf, 1 teaspoon of summer savoury, a crumbled chicken stock cube, 3 tablespoons of tomato concentrate and the previously soaked dried mushrooms. After cooking all this for a few minutes on low heat, the tasting would begin. I can see him now, spoon in hand, eyes closed, cocking his head, with us all watching.

Sometimes he would add ¼ of a teaspoon of oregano, or more salt, or black pepper, or more water or wine, until he was satisfied.

Task completed, he would go and have a nap while we cleaned up: not only utensils and pans, but also splattered windows, stove, sink and floor.

John always made the goulash a day before serving it. That way he was able to take some fat off the top, heat it and taste it again before it went on the table.

Then the drama would start.

John: "Aw, it's not as good as the last one…."

We: "Oh, but it is! Great! Better!" No one was able to fish for compliments better than John, all the while wearing a smug smile, knowing it was damned good…

He liked polenta best as an accompaniment, but mashed potatoes, rice or pasta all go very well with it.

### Goulash JFT

Ingredients for a large pot, feeding 6 -8 people

6 fillets of the neck of lamb

3 large onions

75 g (3 oz.) dried wild mushrooms,
reconstituted in hot water

½ glass of red wine

1 chicken stock cube

3 tablespoons of tomato concentrate

2 tablespoons of fresh paprika

Oil and butter for frying

Salt and pepper

1 bay leaf

½ tsp. summer savoury

### Brussels Sprout Soup

What would England be without Brussels
sprouts! They are served in every restaurant and
cafeteria; they are the staple of school meals
and office canteens.

One night we were invited to a chic dinner
party and the first course was a most delicious
soup. When I inquired of the hostess what sort
of soup it was, she smiled and said: "Nobody
recognizes it! It's Brussels sprout soup!" The
surprise was complete! She told me how to
make it:

### Brussels Sprout Soup

For every 2 lbs. (900g) of Brussels sprouts,
use one clove of garlic and 2 level teaspoons

of your favourite curry powder. Boil in chicken broth until done, adjust seasoning and put through blender, add cream before serving. Et voila, Crème de Choux de Bruxelles. Delicious either with garlic croûtons or hot baguette.

I often bought a 28 lb. (about 12½ kg) bag of Brussels sprouts when we happened to be at a country market on a Saturday and made big quantities of soup for freezing.

### Garlic Croûtons

Á propos of croûtons, do make your own. Get a marrow bone from your butcher, scrape out the marrow, chop it finely and let it melt on low heat in a skillet. Add a little butter, some salt and pepper and a whole clove of peeled garlic. Leave on low heat for another five minutes or so and remove the garlic. Place cubes of wholewheat sandwich bread evenly on the fat, turning the heat up a notch, and let them take colour. Then carefully turn them over with a fork, letting them fry until golden brown. .

## Hachapuri

There seem to be a lot of Hachapuri recipes around. I had almost forgotten how we came by ours, until the children remembered:
Our very favourite au pair was a Finnish school teacher, Sinikka, who took a sabbatical from her village school to come to England and perfect her English.
I had been a little apprehensive about employing a school teacher, thinking she might not want to do any cleaning or dish washing or digging in the garden. How wrong I was! She tackled every job cheerfully and efficiently.

My only regret was that she didn't want to stay another year!
And she introduced us to hachapuri. Her grandmother had taught her how to make it. We changed it slightly, as she used dill, which I'm not very fond of. We substituted it with basil and added a little tomato to the filling. For the dough, use any recipe for soda bread.

**Hachapuri:**
6 cups (a scant 700g) flour
1½ cups (30 cl) buttermilk
1 egg
¼ cup (5 cl) shortening
2 teaspoons of bicarbonate of soda
**Filling:**
½ lb. (225g) Ricotta
1¼ lb. (550g) Feta
½ lb. (225g) Mozzarella
1 teaspoon of freshly ground black pepper
1 egg
1 tomato, deseeded, peeled and chopped
A handful of chopped fresh basil

Make the dough with the ingredients above. Let it rest. Line a deep pie dish with half of the dough, letting it hang over the rim a little. Chop all the cheeses; mix with the egg, tomato, pepper and basil.

Spread this mixture over the dough, place the second half of the dough over it and seal all around the edges. Pierce in several places and bake in a medium oven until it smells done.

## Stuffed Zucchini

Many years ago, in the sixties, we had dinner at a superb Italian restaurant in Mayfair called Tiberio. It was beautifully decorated with large ceramic floor tiles, glass tables and a refreshing fountain in the middle. They had one dish that I particularly liked: stuffed zucchini.

One day I looked up a recipe for this unusual dish. I couldn't find any, so I set an afternoon aside and experimented.

I first looked at scores of recipes for stuffed zucchini. Most of them told you to boil the vegetable first, then stuff and bake it. Since I remembered the zucchini at the Tivoli as being quite crunchy, I didn't want to do that.

I bought four green, shiny zucchini and cut them into 3 inch "logs". Then I sat outside in the sun and proceeded to hollow them out. It took me an hour to get fourteen logs done and ready to stuff.

While preparing different stuffings I stood the logs on a wooden board and placed them on the dishwasher. Then I boiled some Camargue rice in chicken broth. In one bowl I mixed 2 teaspoons of finely chopped rosemary, in another 2 tablespoons of finely chopped fresh sage. I chopped an onion and sautéed it in butter and oil. For meat I originally wanted to use veal, but finally settled on pork loin, which I slowly stewed in its own juice. I also soaked some old bread in lukewarm water.

In the electric mixer I reduced the pork to a

coarse puree, added salt and pepper and divided it into 6 portions.

**I made the following combinations:**

Meat, rice, rosemary

Meat, rice, sage

Meat, rice, onions, rosemary

Meat, rice, onions, sage

Meat, bread (water squeezed out), rosemary

Meat, bread, onions, sage

At this stage Feisty, my cat, decided to come and investigate and jumped on the dishwasher – yep, you guessed it. She tripped on the board and all my carefully prepared logs ended up on the floor. Three of them broke, and I didn't see the cat for the rest of the afternoon.

When I calmed down I stuffed the logs that were left over and lay them into an oven-proof dish, poured concentrated chicken broth over them and baked them in a medium oven for 30 minutes.

Verdict: they all tasted very good.

My preference is meat, rice, onion and rosemary. I have since made it again and alternated green and yellow zucchini, and scored them with a fork to make a pretty pattern.

## Steak Tartare

When John made Steak Tartare he reined us all in to help. One of us had to chop onions and cornichons, another pounded the anchovies in a mortar and pestle, a third had to assemble all the other ingredients: Worcestershire sauce, vinegar, mustard, salt, pepper, Tabasco sauce, etc., and yet another was dispatched to separate the eggs, sliding the yolks carefully into a separate bowl. John in the meantime would place the chopped fillet steak (from Allen's, the butcher's on Mount Street of course) into a large bowl and aerate it with a fork. Then he would arrange the cornichons, capers, onions and anchovies on a wooden board, place the bowl with the egg yolks on one side and the array of condiments on the other.

This was his palette.

Now the artist got to work, incorporating all the ingredients except for the egg yolks into the meat with a fork, tasting, correcting, tasting again, and finally adding the egg yolks. Then one last tasting, after which he heaped the tartare on fresh toast triangles - it was invariably sensational.

## Steak Tartare

Here is an approximation of the ingredients and the amounts for 6 people:

1½ lbs. (roughly 700g) of best ground beef fillet

1 medium onion, very finely chopped

10 cornichons, chopped

½ cup of capers, chopped or whole

1 small can of anchovies, pounded in a mortar

2 tablespoons of olive oil

1 tablespoon of cognac

1 tablespoon of red wine vinegar

1 tablespoon of lemon juice

1 tablespoon of Worcester sauce

1 teaspoon of tomato ketchup

2 dashes of Tabasco sauce

salt and pepper to taste

6 ultra fresh egg yolks

# Discovering Les Micocouliers

After thirty moves in thirty-seven years of married life, my husband and I finally decided to search for a place where we could retire. His profession as a petroleum geologist had required us to relocate frequently and we felt the urge to find a permanent home.

This is how we ended up in the relatively unknown region of France, the Cévennes:

In the spring of 1975, at the end of the skiing season in Switzerland, we decided to drive down to Italy, to the Toscana, with the idea of finding the perfect place to fix up and eventually retire to. Unfortunately, heavy snowfalls kept us from using any of the mountain passes across the Alps and we had to route ourselves via France. The estate agent who had given us the addresses of a couple of properties to look at near Siena suggested that since we had to go through France we might look at the possibility of settling in the Languedoc, the less fashionable part of France between the Rhône and the Spanish border. We thought that was not a bad idea. So down the Rhône valley we drove, past Montélimar and Orange, then turned west and arrived in Lodève that night.

It was an inauspicious beginning. The hotel was a long ways from even getting one star. The odor in the room was appalling, the bed awful, and the dinner inedible. I must say that of the many meals I have had in France over the years, that particular one hit rock bottom.

Things didn't pick up in the morning when we met the local estate agent. Our one prerequisite was that we had to have enough flat land for a tennis court, and enough potential space to accommodate our four children and their present and future families.

Well, we were shown little stone houses with postage stamp gardens, or no gardens at all, and even semi-detached village dwellings.

*Les Micocouliers, 1982*

Very discouraged, we nevertheless went on to meet another agent, Monsieur Durand in the town of Ganges, who showed us another small house with not even enough space to put up a ping-pong table. At least this fellow had the sense to listen to us. "Ah, bon!" he said, "I think I have just the property that might suit you!" He led us to an ancient stone built former silkworm farm in Moulès, near Ganges… and we immediately fell in love with it. There were two buildings, separated by an arbour of Virginia creepers; 14,000 square metres of land and the two dwellings full of charming corners and mysterious cellars. There was a terrace and a courtyard with a bread oven which had obviously been used as a rabbit hutch. There was wild thyme and wild asparagus in the garden, and even a small vineyard.

However, everything had to be renovated, from the roofs to the kitchen. There were no inside bathrooms, and wires hung from the beautiful vaulted 16th century ceiling of the living room. We found old sardine cans and empty Camembert boxes lying around, and a terrible mess everywhere. When we asked our original agent from Lodève what the price was, he said 350,000 francs, which at that time was quite a lot, about $85,000. We tried to hide how excited we were and told him we would think it over.

In the car we talked and talked and found more and more reasons to buy in France instead of Italy. It was nearer to London, where we were living at the time, close to a good international airport (Montpellier), with direct flights to London. The government was surely more stable in France than in Italy; our children all spoke French, whereas only John and I spoke Italian. We were suddenly quite taken with the idea of moving to France. Back in London, we wanted to consider everything at length.

Of course the agent called and said we had better make up our minds quickly, as there was someone else interested in the property, but we refused to be rushed. Two weeks later we decided to fly to Marseille and hire a car in order to look around a little more.

We drove to Ganges and looked at all the estate agents' windows. And there, "our" house was still on display. We went in and spoke to a very nice man, Monsieur Rousselin. We told him that we had gotten the impression that the house had been sold. He was surprised to hear that. No, he said, he had had no other inquiries. Then we expressed our feeling that the price was a bit high at 350,000 French francs. His eyebrows went up and he pulled a printed sheet out of a drawer with the particulars on it. Surprise, surprise, black on white, the price was quoted as 260,000 French francs!!!

To make a long and complicated story short, we got an architect to check whether the

foundations were sound, and when he said yes, we went ahead and purchased the property. The original agent from Lodève actually had the gall to ask for a sales commission! Needless to say, we sent him packing. Thus began our more than thirty years at *Les Micocouliers*, named after the prevalent local trees, known as nettle trees. Many books have been written about the challenges of renovating old houses in France and Italy. Speaking from my own experience, none of them have been exaggerated.

We thought we were being clever by moving a camping van into the courtyard. We would be able to stay there and supervise the renovations until a bedroom and bathroom were ready for occupation in the main house. The builders weren't impressed.

What "mañana" is to the Spaniard and Mexican, "demain, sans faute!" (tomorrow, for sure!) is to the Frenchman in the Midi.

I don't know how I endured those interminable hours and days of waiting for plumbers, electricians, masons and carpenters to show up, but fortunately we were able to count on Ricky, the son of our dear friend Fred Penniman, to keep an eye on the proceedings when we couldn't be around. Eventually our patience was rewarded and we were able to spend the first night under our own new roof.

After a little more than three years, in September of 1978, we decided that the house was in good enough shape to celebrate our 30th wedding anniversary in style. We invited everyone - the workmen, neighbours, friends and relatives from everywhere. There were over 100 people in the end, from all corners of the world.

Our dear friend John Paterson undertook the monumental task of cleaning out the bread oven and lined it with refractory bricks. Our one and only stab at making bread in it convinced us of its impracticality: it took stacks and stacks of wood to get a good bed of embers. We came to understand why bread ovens were only economical when they served the need of a whole community.

Fortunately Chrish, my oldest daughter, brought her cook and maid from Egypt to help with all the work. We dug a pit, bought a whole sheep and barbecued it on a spit. We made gallons of potato salad, roasted kilos and kilos of aubergines, peppers and onions, sliced buckets full of tomatoes for salad, bought 5 litre kegs of wine, and Andrea, my youngest daughter, made one of her renowned cakes. The decorating was in the able hands of my middle daughter, Katrin, who left her decorating business in Houston for a few days to do her magic at Les Micocouliers. We had a bar and a juke box in the cistern room, square trestle tables on the lawn and candles everywhere.

It was truly a perfect party. The weather gods smiled on us and provided an Indian summer night – a southern, deep night sky, lit by what seemed like millions of stars. I don't remember where our Swiss and American and English friends slept, but the next morning saw us all in good shape and fit enough to clean up.

## Pebble Mosaics

When John was semi-retired, he developed all kinds of interests.

He loved to copy the paintings that he admired. Modigliani and Carl Liner were his favourites, but he also "did" Matisse and Renoir. And he loved making his own frames from wood that he found in the local dump.

He got an old window, knocked out the glass and used the panes for picture frames. Being a geologist, though, he never lost his love for rocks and stones. He decided to create a mosaic in the courtyard. He carried home bags and bags of rounded pebbles and pieces of brick that he found in the dry river beds. For two mosaics he used the lozenge motif. He left an empty space in the middle in which to plant flowers.

He surrounded the jujube trees with a similar design.

*John's pebble mosaic*

# Settling down in Moulès

**Having a wonderful vegetable garden and access to so much fresh food has inspired many dishes.**

I especially like to use what's in season to produce simple fare with a little twist, and not spend hours in the kitchen, measuring and stirring and sieving.

Here at Les Micocouliers we have a huge larder which used to be a sheep fold. I love to look at all the shelves filled with preserves: apricot, Concord grape, fig/walnut/green tomato, seedless wild blackberry, strawberry, gooseberry, rose hip jams, crab apple and pomegranate jelly. There are pickled capers, pickled cucumbers and pickled mushrooms; sun-dried tomatoes, relish, saffron onions, spiced peaches, spiced figs, green tomato and fig chutney, black olives and salsas.

There are bottles of different vinegars: red wine, white wine, cider, Balsamic, some with rosemary, some with wild thyme or wild summer savoury. A bag of dried cherries from our own trees, much appreciated by grandchildren for munching on, is hanging on a hook.

Other hooks display branches of bay leaves, wild fennel and verbena, all from my garden. There are linen bags filled with dried summer savoury, wild lavender, wild sage and Roman chamomile, all collected from nearby fields and forests.

## Broccoli

This beneficent vegetable does very well in our Mediterranean climate. In October I put out eight plants. Sometimes they linger and don't do anything for two or even three months, then, all of a sudden small buds appear and turn into florets. The more you pick, the more they produce, well into April.

I am not overly fond of broccoli and have therefore had to devise recipes that tickle my palate.

Picked fresh, broccoli florets (use the stalks for soup) should be immersed into boiling water for not more than 60 seconds, taken out with a slotted spoon and run under cold water to arrest the cooking process.

### Broccoli

Cover a shallow serving dish with the broccoli; add a sliced, roast pepper and some garlic croûtons.
Use your own favourite salad dressing.
The one I like is:
   Rock salt (gros sel) and curried walnut oil.
The big advantage, apart from the exquisite flavour, is that you can serve wine with it. If you use a vinegar-based dressing, the two acids jar.
   For variations, add:
Lardons (fried bacon cubes)
Sliced avocados

Diced, smoked magret de canard (duck breast)
Boiled new potatoes, quartered.

All of these combinations are excellent and a true pleasure for the palate and the eyes.

**Broccoli Soup**
Boil the broccoli stalks, together with a couple of potatoes and a clove of garlic, in chicken broth, and pass through a food mill or purée in the food processor. Serve with croûtons and/or a dollop of cream. For a deliciously different sensation, add a teaspoon of curry powder.

**Green Bean, Onion and Avocado Salad** (*above*)
Top, do not tail, 1 lb. (450g) of small green beans (haricots verts) and boil until al dente. Drain and run them under cold water to stop them from getting too soft. Cut 1 medium onion in half and slice thinly. Place the onions in a shallow dish,

cover with your favorite salad dressing or just coarse sea salt and olive oil. Marinate for an hour, add the green beans and a sliced avocado, toss lightly.

**Andrea's Eggplant and Lamb Salad**
Cube 2 medium eggplants. Place into an oven proof dish and sprinkle 4 tablespoons of olive oil over them.

Roast in a medium hot oven (375F/180°C) for 25 minutes, stirring the bits around to keep them from burning. Set aside.

In a blender combine two small pots of yoghurt, ¾ cups (100g) of diced Feta cheese, a cup of fresh mint, 1 teaspoon of oriental cumin and 1 teaspoon of salt.

Mix the cooled eggplant with 1 lb. (450g) of cooked lamb, cut into bite-size chunks, 20 black olives, 4 tablespoons of roasted pine nuts and ½ cup of chopped dates.

Pour the yoghurt dressing on top and serve on a bed of frizzy endive.

This is a superb luncheon dish and put into plastic containers makes very nice picnic fare.

## Grape Jam Made with Françoise's Italian Grapes

Françoise was our femme de ménage (cleaner/cook/gardener) for 10 years, when we first arrived here in Moulès. She finally left us to take a more regular job at the local hospital. As a sixteen year old Italian bride she followed her husband to live in Ganges, the little market town nearby, about two kilometres from Moulès. She introduced us to many types of wild salad leaves found here, showed us where to find chanterelles and still provides us with Italian grapes from her allotment garden. These are the same as American Concord grapes, and they make the best seedless jam, which I prefer to clear jelly.

Concord grapes are an old acquaintance of mine. When I arrived from Switzerland as a young bride in Massachusetts in 1948, my father-in-law had an enormous harvest of Concord grapes so we decided to put a table in the front yard and sell them. It was a strange experience for me! In Switzerland, certainly at that time, you would neither be allowed nor would the neighbours approve of such an unorthodox way of hawking your wares.

Our next-door neighbour, Mrs. Howes, showed me how to make the jam.

### Mrs. Howes's Grape Jam

Pick the grapes off the stems and place them in a heavy-bottomed saucepan. Add enough water to cover the grapes by ½ inch (1.25 cm). Boil them rapidly for 4 minutes. Mash them with a potato masher. Put them through a food mill (or a strainer), using the finest of the three blades. The skins and pips will stay behind and you get a thickish juice. For each cup (20 cl) of liquid, add ¾ (15 cl) cup pre-warmed sugar. Boil at a gallop until the mixture starts to drop heavily from a wooden spoon. Place 1 teaspoon of the jam on a cold plate. When it sets, it is ready.

Bottle in sterilized jars. Screw the tops on tightly, put the jars upside down for a few minutes, then back upright, doing this 2 or 3 times. This jam goes especially well with pancakes.

## Stuffed Peppers, Eggplant, and Zucchini

Françoise of the grape jam fame also made a sensational dish of stuffed aubergines, peppers and zucchini. It did take her most of an afternoon, but it was well worth it. When she served an enormous platter of these goodies there would arise an mmh… and oh and ah all around the table. This is how she made them: .

### Stuffed Peppers, Eggplant, and Zucchini à la Françoise

4 eggplants
2 red peppers
2 green peppers
2 yellow zucchini
2 green zucchini

For the stuffing:
1 ½ lbs. (675g) of sausage meat (she was very particular, only one butcher had the right kind)
Half a stale baguette,

soaked in cold water

3 eggs

3 cloves of garlic

A handful of chopped basil

A handful of chopped Italian, flat leaf parsley

**For the sauce:**

4 large tomatoes

2 tablespoons of chopped onions

2 tablespoons of chopped basil

1 garlic clove, pushed through the garlic press

1 teaspoon of salt

½ teaspoon of brown sugar

Fry the sausage meat for a couple of minutes to

render the fat, which you discard. Mix with the rest of the ingredients, the bread having had the water squeezed out of it as much as possible.

Check for salt. Some sausage meat is salty enough to carry everything with it.

Prepare the vegetables by cutting them in half lengthways and discarding the seeds and membranes of the peppers and hollowing out the aubergines and the zucchini.

Make a tomato sauce with the peeled fresh tomatoes, the onion and some chopped basil, ½ a teaspoon of brown sugar, salt and pepper. Purée.

Place the vegetables in a big oven-proof platter or roasting pan. Spoon the stuffing into them. Pour the tomato sauce around them and bake them in a 350F (175°C) oven until they smell done.

**Sweet Pickles**

Put 6-8 medium unpeeled cucumbers through the slicer. Place in a large roasting pan (*left*).

Add 2 sliced green peppers, 3 sliced onions and 3 chopped cloves of garlic. Cover with ½ a cup of *gros sel* (rock salt) and ice cubes. Place in fridge overnight. Next day put the mixture into a colander and let the liquid drain off. In a large saucepan bring to a boil: 3 cups (400g) of brown sugar, 3 cups (60 cl) of cider vinegar, 1½ teaspoons of curry powder, 1½ teaspoons of mustard powder and 2 teaspoons of celery seeds.

Add the cucumber mixture, bring back to a quick boil and decant into sterilized jars. The pickles are ready as soon as they have cooled off (*below left*).

If you purée the pickles in a blender you'll get the most delicious hot-dog relish.

# Dog Walks

My garden is large, but I nevertheless like to take Tess for a walk in the woods and the neighbouring vineyards. I need the exercise as much as she does.

In the summer the sun hits the courtyard in the morning. When I return from the walk, I come in through the old wrought-iron gates from west to east and see the ancient cobblestones glistening, trying to tell me about all the carriages that have rolled over them, all the feet that have trod on them, and all the people that have swept them… Nowadays I use an outdoor vacuum cleaner to get rid of leaves and other débris. I never come back from dog walks with empty hands.

In winter I collect wood and pine cones for the ever hungry fireplaces.

From March on there are early flowers, wild iris and bee orchids. April and May bring wild garlic, wild salads, bright blue borage blossoms to scatter on salad, camomile flowers to dry and elder flowers for cordial.

## Wild Garlic and Ham Sandwich

Wild garlic appears around the middle of April. The sun is already warm, but evenings can be chilly, and since the house has very thick walls it takes a long time to reach eighteen or nineteen centigrade in the living room.

A fire in the evening is therefore a must and I gather kindling wood when I take Tess for a walk behind Ginestous, a large property up the valley a ways. Small cade (a very calorific type of cedar) twigs and some sawn off bigger logs are what I am gathering. I then sit down in the sun near the ancient menhirs and have a ham sandwich, liberally stuffed with leaves of wild garlic. It turns an ordinary picnic into an original and very tasty one.

The old people here (look who's talking…) attribute lots of great qualities to wild garlic. It is supposed to clean out winter staleness in all the organs and strengthen the blood for the coming summer. It has a pretty, white, sometimes pale pink, blossom, similar to chives, which can be added to salad for a nice effect.

From the last days of May on I gather huge bouquets of wild mauve Phlomis and pick a few cherries on old abandoned cherry trees. When it starts to get hot in the summer, I go out very early and often surprise butterflies still asleep on a flower, their wings neatly folded. I wonder why lepidopterists don't catch their prey in the early morning. One can just pick them off, like berries, instead of hopping around with muslin nets. More romantic, I suppose. Later it's time for wild strawberries, blackberries, the first chanterelles and puff balls. The crab apples turn a beautiful Bordeaux red and inspire me to make crab apple jelly.

### Crab Apple Jelly

Wash the ripe crab apples, remove the stems and the fly and cut into quarters. Place in a heavy bottomed sauce pan and cover with water. Add a whole clove or two. Simmer them until they are soft, but don't stir them. Strain through butter muslin. For each cup of juice use ¾ cups of sugar. Boil until it forms "heavy" drops on a wooden spoon. Pour into clean, hot jars, screw the lid on and turn them upside down for a minute, then right them again.
Serve with pork roast or baked ham.

Meanwhile vine leaves are turning russet and golden, and the harvest is over. Since the grapillons, small bunches of grapes, are not picked, I can munch on grapes into November.

## Spider Web Day

This is one of the many magical things that occur here. About three times a year these particular spiders seem to get on the phone to each other and decide to weave their webs overnight. There are two kinds of spider webs. One kind sits on the ground and is between two and six inches (five to fifteen centimeters) across with a hole in the middle, like a funnel, presumably to catch the unsuspecting insect which will be sucked down into it. The other kind hangs between branches of grapevines or stalks of tall grass. The webs are

*Spider web and bee orchids*

always beautifully woven and have raindrops on them that look either very pure, like diamonds, or have a slight opaque rim around them, like moonstones. You never see just one of these webs, there are thousands of them. And the next day they are gone!
Spring is altogether a wonderful time of the year in this region. The bee orchids start to bloom, first the chocolate coloured ones, feigning a bee, then the flatter yellow ones, showing a black fly on its petals. The last one to make its appearance is the mauve variety. Yellow and purple iris pop up, not very big, but lots of them.

*Salsify flower and seed*

## Salsify, Flower and "Parachute" Seeds

The wild salsify, or goat's beard, has an exquisite flower. The centre is yellow and the outer petals are in different shades of mauve, sometimes flecked with yellow, all contained by spiky green leaves. It looks like a multi-coloured star, but unfortunately it shuts up tight as soon as you take it inside. Alas, it only blooms for one day, like the caper flower, but after staying closed for a few days it then metamorphoses and bursts into a globe of delicate "parachutes", as we used to call them as children, the seeds that float away to find a new home.

And of course the cuckoos make their début. I have kept track of the cuckoo calls for many years and in different countries, and they all "cuckoo" within a half tone of each other, starting with an almost clean minor third, f-d, getting between ¼ and ½ tone lower towards the end of the season. I carry a tuning-fork in my pocket from the first of April onwards in order to check all the cuckoo calls.

This is a region that grows literally bushes of wild snap dragons. There are sometimes up to 25 tall stems on a plant, deep pink to purple in colour, breath-taking. I have transplanted loads of them successfully into my garden. They reseed themselves into every nook and cranny, springing up miraculously out of a little hole in the old grey stone walls.

At this time of the year the path in my garden which leads out to the compost heap is a riot of colours, deep purple stock, bright red poppies, yellow Escholzia and pink snap dragons, all framed by lush green foliage.

On the culinary front, local green asparagus start to get affordable. They are fat, juicy and full of flavour. There are also lots of wild ones, much smaller and thinner, but very tasty.

If you are not cooking the asparagus as soon as you get home, keep them fresh by placing them in a jar of water, like flowers. The same goes for artichokes, if you buy them with their stalks.

## Asparagus

**My favourite way of preparing them is this:**
Peel the asparagus from about a third of the way down and break off the white ends. Cook very carefully in salted water until the hardest, lowest part of the stem is al dente. Drain and serve warm with curried walnut oil and rock salt.

**Daniel's Asparagus and Cheese Gratin** (*opposite*)
Prepare the asparagus like above.
Cool them in cold water to keep them from getting too soft.
Put the tougher stalks in a pot with an onion, quartered, and 4 cloves of garlic.
   Bring to a boil and keep at a lively simmer for about 12 minutes. Strain and return the stock to

the pan.
Boil down to ½ cup (10 cl).

Pour in a generous ½ cup (10 cl) of cream,
1 teaspoon of strong mustard and cook
the sauce at a roaring boil until you have
about one cup (20 cl) of a fairly thick sauce.
Season cautiously with salt and pepper.

Make a crumble by combining a couple
of handfuls of bread crumbs with ½
cup of grated strong cheddar and
Parmesan, and a dollop of butter.

Arrange the boiled asparagus
on either individual serving
plates or one big serving dish.
Pour the sauce over and
sprinkle with a generous
amount of the crumble.

Place under a hot grill
until the crumble browns
and the cheese begins to
melt. Serve immediately.

## Dried Flowers

Even on the hottest days
of July and August, I
come back from the
dog walk with bounty.
Euphorbia, which is the
bane of the vegetable
garden, turns a delicate
coral shade. The wild carrot
produces gorgeous large
flowers with a little garnet jewel
in the middle.
The wild leeks have now shot up
and you can see their pretty clusters

of dried flowers from afar.
They add stature to any composition of
dried flowers and keep for years.
There is also a nasty
type of weed
of the

wart family that manages to transform itself into a darkish, brick-coloured beauty, a lovely contrast to the beige wild leek.

We have nine types of thistles here that I know of. Some have very pointy, sharp spikes *(left)*. The flowers of the largest one becomes downy white, like a cushion, and grasshoppers and cicadas love to snooze on them.

A smaller, very spiky one manages to produce very pretty plumbago-coloured heads, but most of them have purple or yellow flowers. The most famous thistle of course is the artichoke.

As kids, when we were on holiday in the Alps, we'd learn the intricate art, with the help of a pocket knife, of laboriously extricating the edible part of the silver thistle, now a highly protected species.

Up on the high plateau near here, the Causses, you see these same silver thistles nailed to barn doors as a weather vane. When they are flat, it's a good weather sign. When the leaves curl up, it's going to rain.

## Artichokes

Of all the hundreds of ways of preparing artichokes, my favourite, whether I use the small purple ones or the large globe artichokes, is the following:

I boil them in plenty of water in which I have placed a wedge of lemon, peppercorns, a bay leaf and some rock salt, until al dente.

Do not overcook!

Serve with the wonderfully tasty curried walnut oil as dressing.

Some years ago I planted a row of artichokes up against a lovely stone wall in order to enjoy the purple flowers with the grey background. When a friend of mine, whose name shall go unmentioned, was visiting, she made the round of the garden and came back with a dozen artichokes in her apron. "These would have gone into flower if I hadn't picked them", she announced proudly…

# North African Specialties

The following recipes come from the Maghreb, North Africa. I tasted most of these dishes for the first time at a gathering of "pieds-noirs", the French people who used to live in North Africa and reluctantly had to leave their sometimes huge properties behind to start a new life in France.

They get together quite often, reminisce, complain, and regale each other with food from là-bas.

Every first Sunday in October they organize a big méchoui, whole mutton cooked on a spit. The preparations begin the day before. A ditch is dug, big enough to accommodate a contraption that can hold two beasts. The next morning at 5am, the stalwarts go and make a fire with holm oak. By 8am they have lovely embers and the spit is ready for use.

The venue for this gathering is superb: the grounds of an old monastery, La Gardiole, near St. Hippolyte-le-Fort.

Huge oaks provide shade, and trestle tables are covered with the dishes that people bring. Each family has its own favourite Moroccan or Tunisian or Algerian speciality which they proudly display.

Around three o'clock, most of the food has disappeared, large quantities of wine have helped it along, latest news has been exchanged, and the pétanque competitions begin. This is a similar game to the Italian boccia, popular around here as it doesn't require a prepared piste. Any reasonably flat area will do. It is played with metal balls and the object of the game is to send your ball as closely to the *cochonet* (literally, little pig), a small brown disc, as possible and dislodge the balls of your opponents, if they are closer to it than yours.

I owe many recipes to this pieds-noirs get-together. Here is a selection:

### Chickpeas, Onions, Tuna and Mint

Soak 1 lb. (450g) of good quality chickpeas overnight. Place 1 cup of very finely chopped sweet onions into a bowl, add 1 cup of also very finely chopped mint. Add ¼ lb. (110g) of drained, canned tuna fish. Mix together. Boil the chickpeas with one head of unpeeled garlic and half a teaspoon of salt until done, but don't let them get mushy. Drain. Mix with all the other ingredients *while warm!* Add ¼ cup (5 cl) olive oil, double that if you use tuna fish canned in water.

(If you can get fresh tuna, use it, boiled in the following manner:

Put a slice of tuna in a tight-fitting saucepan, cover with water. Add half a lemon, a sprig of rosemary, two sprigs of parsley and a handful of fennel tops. Simmer for 3 or 4 minutes. You want the fish to be

almost raw. Leave it to cool in its broth.
Remove skin and bones and the very dark parts.
Adjust for salt).
Even non-lovers of tuna like this dish!

### Chickpeas with Eggplant and Carvi
Prepare the chickpeas as above. Mix with chunks of fried aubergines. Sprinkle 3 tablespoons of carvi (North African cumin) over the whole dish. Adjust for salt.

## Aubergine Spread (Baba Ghanouj)
The Spanish do a very similar spread which they serve as tapas, their famous little hors d'oeuvre dishes.

When I tasted the one at the pieds-noirs gathering, it had a slightly different flavour, really more oriental. I managed to find the lady who had brought it, and this is what she told me:
Be sure to always grill the eggplant over a charcoal fire. Baking it in the oven doesn't give it that smoky, outdoorsy perfume. Prepare it at least one day ahead of consumption to enable the spices to penetrate the rather bland taste of the aubergine.
And the one ingredient that I never saw in any other recipe: harissa, the North African hot pepper paste.
So here is how she does it:

## Aubergine Spread

Pierce and grill 3 or 4 shiny eggplants, not so close to the charcoal as to burn them. Turn them occasionally. This should take about 40 minutes, depending on the thickness of the fruit.

Next to the eggplant on the grill, place a small fireproof dish in which you put 4 large, unpeeled cloves of garlic (more if you really like garlic).

Let cool. Cut aubergines in half and scoop out the flesh. Squeeze the garlic out of its skin. Pound the eggplant and garlic to a smooth pulp, add 2 tablespoons of olive oil, half a cup of fresh coriander leaves, ½ to ¾ cup of tahini (sesame seed paste), 1 teaspoon of harissa, 2 teaspoons of lemon juice and salt. Mix thoroughly with a fork.

Put in a jar and pour 1 teaspoon of olive oil over the top. Serve the next day with pita bread, tortilla triangles or potato chips.

This spread lends itself to numerous variations. Let your imagination guide you! Cumin, chopped onions, parsley, chives come to mind.

## Josephine's Anchoyade

Josephine lived in Morocco for twenty two years and her anchoyade always disappears within ten minutes of being put on the table. It is so simple to make: Pound good quality canned anchovies with garlic and olive oil or put the ingredients in a food processor. Serve on thinly sliced baguette.

## Deep Fried Cheese Meringues

6 egg whites
½ lb. (225g) grated Gruyère cheese
Beat the egg whites with a pinch of salt until *very* stiff.
Incorporate the cheese very carefully.
Add a pinch of nutmeg.

With a spoon form dumplings and deep fry them in good quality oil. Dry on paper towels. These taste delicious hot, lukewarm or cold.

# Le Bon Poulet

**This should have been the most perfect evening. Late summer, friends who have a lovely little house near a brook, a big vegetable garden across the street and a small vineyard up behind the house.**

We had met at a local garden centre and became acquainted via food, our principal conversation piece. We swapped recipes: I gave them the proportions for crumble mixture; they told me how to make crèpes Suzette. One day, they invited us for dinner. They wanted us to get to know some other English speaking people in the area.

It turned out to be an especially hot day. Even at 8 pm, when we arrived, it was quite stifling. We were surprised to see that all the windows and doors were shut tightly.

Surely there was no air conditioning in this out of the way hamlet? No, of course not, but they maintained that it was hotter out than in, and that insects would come in if we left the windows open.

My hope of sitting out on the back terrace vanished when we were escorted past a heavily laden dining room table into the "salon".

The coffee table was covered with every conceivable type of wine and liquor. From red and white wines via Martini Rosso and Bianco, sherry, Cartagène, Souze, to bourbon, vodka, scotch, gin and various brandies. The other guests arrived, English and equipped with about twenty words of French. Since our hosts spoke no English, John and I were of course kept busy translating.

And still no air.

Having more people in the small house raised the temperature even higher. When I couldn't stand it any more, I opened the balcony door and the first creatures to shoot outside were two cats, stretching themselves out on the relatively cool tiles of the terrace.

And so to dinner.

They had pulled out all the stops for us: Three glasses at each cover, heavy silverware, silver candelabra, huge linen napkins (formal French dinner napkins more than cover your whole lap), in short, the works.

To begin with they served saumon en croûte (salmon in puff pastry), really delicious, if perhaps not ideal for a hot summer's night. Then we had a beautifully presented golden yellow chicken in onion and cider sauce, superb, accompanied by a purée de pommes de terre. Suddenly, horror of horrors, a wasp was spotted on the wall. The master of the house rushed out, got a can of insecticide (une bombe!) and proceeded to cover the insect with its contents.

Never mind that the dining-room was very small and never mind that half the insecticide fell on the food… the wasp must be gotten rid of. Success!

Somehow I had a hard time eating anything after that – which was just as good, as that gave me time to translate stories from French into English and English into French.

The best thing about that evening was the chicken recipe which I got from the French lady.

## Chicken Smothered in Onions and Cider Vinegar

Slowly fry four large, thinly sliced Cévennes onions in butter and oil until very soft. Be patient and don't let them burn.

In the meantime brown a chicken on all sides and place into a tight fitting casserole, just big enough to accommodate the chicken and some sauce. The onions should not just accompany the chicken, but *smother* it.

When the onions are done, add one heaped tablespoon of turmeric. This gives it that lovely golden colour and is, incidentally, a powerful anti-oxidant. Pour 1½ (30 cl) cups of cider vinegar over the onions, crumble a chicken stock cube over the concoction and cook for 5 minutes or so. Check for salt. Pour this sauce over the chicken, cover and cook slowly until the chicken is done.

Serve on rice, much better than mashed potatoes. Like most onion dishes, it is even better the next day. And an additional hint: if you cook this chicken the day before serving, put it in the fridge. The fat will have risen to the top by next morning and you can remove most of it and also some of the skin.

## Chicken with Curried Walnut Oil

In a small bowl, combine 4 tablespoons of walnut oil with 1 teaspoon of curry and 2 teaspoons of turmeric. Brush a chicken with this mixture and brown it in a tablespoon of corn oil and a walnut size piece of butter. Place in a casserole that is just big enough for the chicken plus 10-16 small potatoes and has a tight fitting lid. French "rattes" potatoes are ideal, but any small, firm potato will do. Red ones don't take on the yellow colour as well. Brush the potatoes with the spiced walnut oil. Put them around the chicken. Sprinkle 2

*Chicken with curried walnut oil*

Bake in a moderate oven (160°C) until it smells done. Remove the foil and bake for another 10 minutes.

This is delicious hot, lukewarm or cold. When you have it cold, a luscious golden jelly forms around the chicken pieces, a real treat. Wonderful for picnics, but bring plenty of paper towels or napkins.

tablespoons of rock salt and another teaspoon of turmeric over chicken and potatoes. Cover with a tight lid and bake in a 350F (175°C) oven for 1½ hours. Baste three or four times with the liquid which accumulates at the bottom of the casserole. This is a visual and culinary feast and so easy to prepare.

### Lemon and Garlic Chicken

Cut one chicken for every 4 persons into portions. Place in a shallow casserole. Scrub an organic lemon and finely shave off the rind with a vegetable peeler. Cut the rind into little strips. Halve the lemon and squeeze its juice over the chicken. Add 2 teaspoons of finely chopped garlic, 1 teaspoon of turmeric, 1 teaspoon of black pepper, 2 teaspoons of rock salt and the lemon zest. Sprinkle with about 2 tablespoons of olive oil. Cover the whole thing with aluminum foil and let marinate for at least a couple of hours at room temperature.

### Best Chicken Salad

Sauté 3 tablespoons of finely chopped onions in one tablespoon of oil and one teaspoon of butter until soft. Moisten with a cup (20 cl) of dry white wine and a cup (20 cl) of water. Add ½ a bay leaf, 3 parsley stalks, 1 clove of garlic and 1 teaspoon of mild curry powder. Simmer for a few minutes to reduce the quantity by half. Strain and cool. Incorporate 1 tablespoon of quince jelly into 2 cups of mayonnaise. Mix with the liquid and 2 lbs. (900g) of cooked chicken, cut into bite size chunks. Check for salt and adjust if necessary.

### Second Best Chicken Salad

Cut a plump fennel bulb in half, leaving some of the dark green fronds on. Count half a bulb per person. Slice the long way. Arrange on a platter, alternating fennel and slices of cold chicken. Sprinkle gros sel (rock salt) on top, squeeze lemon juice over and finish with curried olive oil. Yummy!

# Brunch

After an early morning excursion to the local Friday marché, or on a lazy Sunday, we like to throw together a little brunch. Part of the fun of living here is using impromptu ingredients in old and established recipes.

Look around the garden and beyond and you find inspiration. A handful of spinach or dandelions, fresh wild garlic leaves give these tuna patties from our Irish friend Daniel a special flavour. Daniel came into our life when he rented a gîte (B&B) in the house next to ours. He is a terrific cook and the many Sunday dinners and summer evening dinner parties which he gave when he moved into his own house are memorable both for their content and their artistic presentation.
Sadly he sold the house and moved to Budapest, but his recipes have a special place in our culinary life.

**Daniel's Pork and Spinach Terrine** (*below*)
2 lbs. (900g) pork belly or any kind of pork
12 ounces (330g) of bacon
½ lb. (225g) pork liver
2 onions
2/3 cloves of garlic
2 eggs
3 cups of cooked or frozen spinach leaves
herbs (rosemary, thyme, parsley, etc.)
nutmeg
pepper and salt to taste

Roughly process ingredients in a blender. This will make 2 loaf pans full.
Bake in a moderate oven for between 1 and 1½ hours, until a tooth pick comes out clean.
Take it out of the oven and, while still hot, protect the top with saran wrap and weight it down. This gets rid of excess liquid and will slice better.

**Daniel's Fish Cakes**
Cut skin and bones off a nice thick slice of fresh tuna. Chop roughly and put in blender together with a medium size boiled potato, an onion, 2 tablespoons of bread crumbs, one egg, 2 handfuls of cooked spinach or dandelions, 2

tablespoons each of finely cut wild garlic leaves and flat leaved parsley, ½ teaspoon of cumin, 2 gratings from the nutmeg grater, salt and pepper to taste. Blend and form into patties, dust with flour and fry 2 minutes on each side. Lovely for a special Sunday breakfast, accompanied by:

### Daniel's Hot Salsa

2 cups deseeded, peeled and
  chopped, very ripe tomatoes
4 red peppers
2 fresh chili peppers,
  deseeded and finely chopped
1 ¼ (160g) cups brown sugar
3 tablespoons of walnut vinegar
3 tablespoons of Balsamic vinegar
1 teaspoon of grated ginger
1 teaspoon of ground cumin
1 teaspoon of ground coriander

Grill, peel and chop the red peppers
  Put half of the peppers, 1 cup of the tomatoes, the chili peppers and the spices through a blender. Warm the vinegar with the sugar, add the mix from the blender and let it come to a boil. Reduce the heat, add the rest of the tomatoes and red peppers and simmer for about 30 minutes. Put into sterilized jars, screw the lids on and turn upside down for a few minutes, then right them. This is a wonderful accompaniment to roast ham and all cold cuts.

## Cheese Pie

Every seven or eight weeks we have what we call "le pot" at our local bridge club. Members bring things to eat and the club offers the beverages.
I always bring a cheese pie and it disappears like the proverbial butter in the sun.

### Cheese Pie

Line a 9 inch (22cm) pie pan with your favourite pie pastry (I use ready-made puff pastry). Preheat oven to 350F (175°C).
  In a bowl combine 3 cups (about 300 g) of mixed grated cheese (cheddar, Swiss, a little Parmesan), one whole egg, 4 tablespoons of cream, ½ a teaspoon of nutmeg and ½ a teaspoon of my magic spice (page 119). Place in the pie pan and bake for about 35 minutes, or until it is nice and brown and smells delicious!

## Huevos Rancheros

A great brunch recipe from Chris and Arnold Gregg from California. They have been stalwart friends and visitors to Les Micocouliers for twenty-five years and have seen the evolution of the house and the garden.

### Huevos Rancheros

Olive oil and corn oil
8 corn tortillas
2 24 oz. cans of stewed tomatoes
4 red and 4 yellow peppers cut into large strips
2 – 3 green chilis (mild)
2 large onions, sliced
one bunch fresh chopped coriander
one bunch chopped flat leaf parsley
1 tsp. ground cumin
8 small eggs
1 bunch chopped chives
16 oz. (450g) combination of shredded

Cheddar, Jack and Mozzarella cheese.
Fry the onions and all the peppers in olive oil until they are wilted. Add half of the coriander and parsley. Strain the stewed tomatoes and chop into bite sized pieces. Reserve the liquid. Put stewed tomatoes into a serving dish. Pour in one half cup of the strained stewed tomato juice, and mix in the peppers. Add ground cumin, salt and pepper to taste.

Crack the eggs into the mixture, making sure that you space the eggs evenly. Use a teaspoon to make pockets for the eggs. Bake at 350F (175c) for 15 – 20 mins until eggs are done.

Meanwhile fry the corn tortillas in hot corn oil until crisp and lightly browned; drain on paper towels and keep warm.

Remove dish from oven and sprinkle with the cheese. Put under the grill until cheese is melted.

To serve, put one corn tortilla on each plate. Scoop out one egg with tomato/ cheese mixture and put on top of tortilla. Garnish with chopped fresh coriander and chives. Serve black beans and salsa on the side.

## Brie en Croûte

This is a hit no matter when you serve it, but it lends itself nicely to a brunch, especially if you balance it with a lot of nice fresh fruit.

### Chrish's Brie en Croûte

One whole medium size Brie cheese
1 lb. (450g) puff pastry
2 oz. (50g) dried wild mushrooms
½ cup white wine for reconstituting mushrooms
1 clove garlic, finely chopped
1 onion, finely chopped

*Huevos Rancheros,*
*ready for baking*

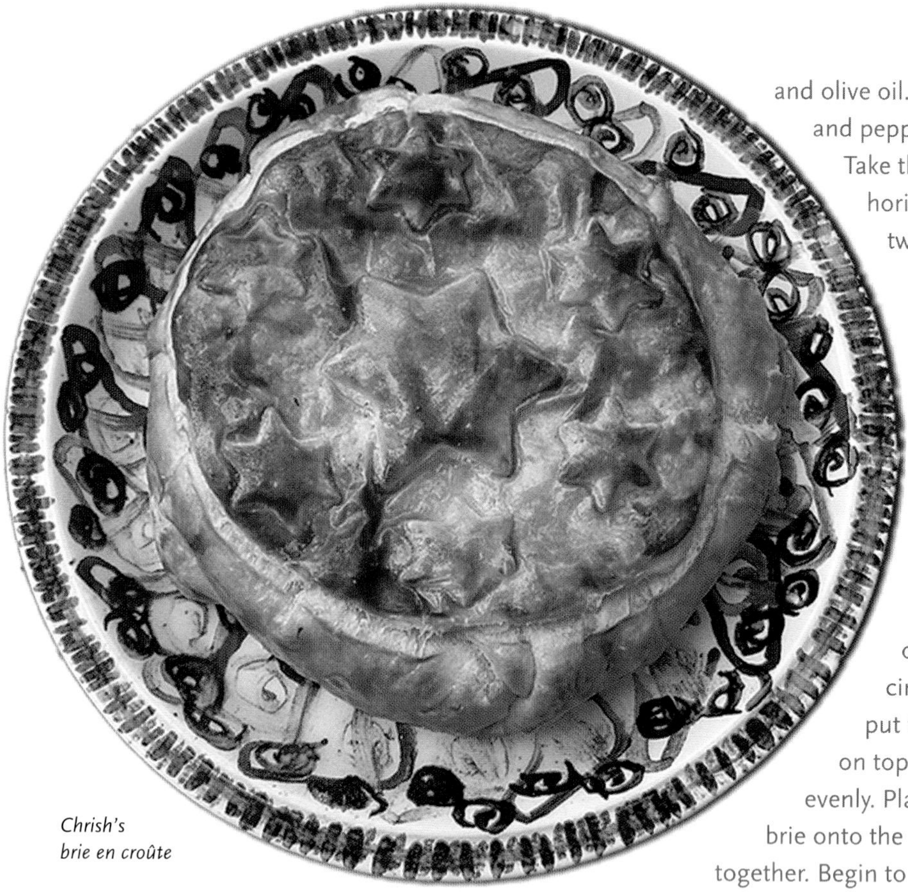

*Chrish's*
*brie en croûte*

1 tablespoon butter
Chopped parsley
2 tablespoons olive oil
½ tablespoon dried thyme
1 egg yolk, whisked, for the glaze

Place the entire brie in the refrigerator
to cool and harden a little.

Reconstitute the dried mushrooms by soaking
them in a mixture of the white wine and an equal
amount of hot water. When they are fully plumped,
drain and chop them finely. Sauté the mushrooms,
together with the onion and garlic, in the butter

and olive oil. Season with thyme, salt
and pepper. Set aside to cool.
Take the brie and slice it
horizontally so you have
two equal wheels.

Roll out the puff pastry
and make two circles:
one approximately three
inches (7.5 cm) wider
in diameter than the
brie; the other should
be the exact size of
the brie. Leave enough
pastry for decoration.

Place the lower half
of the brie on the larger
circle of puff pastry and
put the mushroom stuffing
on top of it, spreading around
evenly. Place the top half of the
brie onto the mixture, and press gently
together. Begin to wrap the edges of the
puff pastry around the top of the brie, then place
the smaller circle on top of that, moistening
the edges with water to *glue* it together. You
will have a nice packet. Brush with egg yolk,
and decorate with the remaining puff pastry.

You can cut out a heart shape or leaves,
or even the initial of one of your guests.
Make sure to also glaze the decoration and
attach it firmly with a little cold water on the
pastry, as it will puff up during baking.

Bake your brie en croûte at 375F (185°C) on
an oiled cookie sheet for about 35 minutes,
or until the pastry is puffy and golden.

# Other Capers

We had been living here for more than 2 years before we discovered that we had a caper bush.

It was hidden behind brambles (of which there was an abundance), but a sharp eyed neighbour spotted it and told me what it was and how to preserve the buds.

You must pick capers before they flower, but fortunately you always miss some, so you can see the exquisite caper flower in all its splendour. Sadly, it only lasts one day. Pickling the buds is simplicity itself.

### Pickling Capers

Dissolve 2 level teaspoons of coarse sea salt (gros sel) in ¾ cup (15 cl) of hot water, add 2 cups (40 cl) of alcohol vinegar and let cool off. Place the capers into a mason jar and pour the vinegar mixture on top. Cover with a triple thickness of butter muslin which you push down on the capers. Fresh capers are buoyant and you have to make sure they stay in the vinegar mixture. Seal the jar. The capers will be ready in about three weeks and keep for over a year.

I have tried different, more expensive vinegars, but find that this ordinary white vinegar suits them best. My Belgian friend Fred suggested preserving capers by covering them in rock salt. He has seen it done in Italy.

I tried a jar full, but found them very salty. If you have an unlimited supply of capers you can experiment with all kinds of ideas, such as:

### Pasta Salad

Big yawn. Everybody makes pasta salad. But this one is especially colourful and tasty, great for feeding a hungry crowd.

It can be prepared the day before, except for the hard boiled egg garnish.

1 cup roast red peppers, sliced
Optional: chopped parsley
and/or chopped basil.

Boil the pasta in salted water
until al dente, drain, mix with all
the ingredients in a large bowl and
drip 1 cup of your favourite salad
dressing over it.
Garnish with quartered
hard boiled eggs

### Tomato Salad
### with Capers and Mint ( *left*)

Slice ripe tomatoes and arrange
prettily on a platter. Sprinkle with
chopped mint and capers. Use
a very simple salad dressing,
for example, olive oil, wine
vinegar and rock salt (*gros sel*) or
walnut oil with balsamic vinegar and rock salt.

### Pasta Salad

For 4 to 6 people, use
1¼ lbs. (500g) of curly red/green/white pasta.
Prepare the other ingredients before you
boil the pasta, so you can incorporate
them into the pasta while it is hot and
absorbs the different flavours better.
Ingredients:
10 cornichons, chopped
1 cup of capers
20 black olives
1 cup of cheese, Cheddar or Cantal,
cut into squares
1 cup of diced ham
½ cup sun-dried tomatoes, chopped

### Superior Potato Salad

While you are boiling some waxy potatoes,
prepare the following dressing:
Slice and fry one large onion until soft,
but don't burn. Combine with ½ cup (10 cl)
of mayonnaise, ¾ cup (15 cl) of olive oil, 2
tablespoons of German mustard, 1/3 cup
(7 cl) of red wine vinegar, 1 tablespoons of salt,
2 chicken stock cubes dissolved in ¼ cup (5 cl)
of boiling water, and ½ cup of capers. Pound a
couple of teaspoons of grilled coriander seeds in
a mortar and pestle and add to the mixture.
Slice the peeled potatoes while hot and pour

the dressing over them, mix carefully. You don't want vinegary mashed potatoes.

**Tartar Sauce**

To accompany breaded fish filets, make (or buy) a mayonnaise.

Dice a big boiled potato and 2 or 3 boiled carrots. Add a cup of boiled green peas and a cup of drained capers. Fold all the ingredients carefully into the mayonnaise.

**Raie au Beurre Noir**
**et aux Câpres**

Buy about ½ lb. (225g) of skate per person.

Simmer the fish in water with the addition of ½ a squeezed lemon and one tablespoon of white wine vinegar.

A few white peppercorns and a sprig of thyme are usually recommended, but John thought

they didn't make the slightest difference. He insisted on ultra-fresh butter and lots of capers.

When the fish was barely done (less than ten minutes) he placed it in buttered waxed paper and kept it warm. In a large frying pan he melted a generous amount, almost ¼ lb. (about 100g), of fresh unsalted butter. Just before it started to burn he added 1½ cups of our own capers, drained, turned the heat down slightly and cooked them until crisp.

He transferred the fish onto a pre-warmed platter and poured the butter/caper sauce over it. Some recipes call for more vinegar, but since the capers are preserved in vinegar, John maintained that that was enough. The fish shouldn't taste like pickles.

*The weekly marché in Ganges, top,*
*and caper flower, left*

81

# Onions

**The Cévennes is an important onion growing region. In every little valley there are acres and acres of terraces, where either rayollettes or oignons de Lézignan are cultivated. The former keep better, the latter are sweeter.**

Both lend themselves to some truly great dishes. They are pulled in September and in October a jolly onion festival takes place in St. Martial, up in the Cévennes mountains. There you can buy tresses of onions and also taste many local onion dishes, like Pissaladière, an onion tart, very similar to the famous Zibelechueche, onion pie, of Switzerland.

### Onion Tart

For a basic Onion Tart, fry 4 or 5 large onions, sliced thinly, in butter and oil until golden. In the meantime make your favourite pie pastry or use ready-made puff pastry.

Stir an egg into the tepid onions, add 2 tablespoons of cream, salt and pepper, a dash of nutmeg. Pour into the uncooked pastry shell and bake until brown.

For a different version, add fried bacon cubes or diced ham and proceed as above. You can also add grated cheese, which will turn your onion pie into a Schafhuuser Zibelechueche, or a cup of chopped, cooked spinach, which will make it a Grüeni Zibelewäihe.

### Confiture d'Oignons

There must be one hundred different combinations for this onion relish. They are all good and make a perfect accompaniment for cold cuts, liver pâtés, foie gras, cheese raclette, meat loaf, pork roast, roast pheasant, venison….

I have perused so many recipes for this, cooked so many versions, tasted so many variations, I hardly know where to start.

Even the way to cut them is not agreed on by everyone. Some slice thinly, some chop. Some quarter and some cut the onion across, but not all the way, so the onion remains partially intact. Some use sharp onions, some red onions, and some little white ones, but I am concerned here with the local sweet onions.

### Confiture d'Oignons

For a one litre size mason jar slice 4-5 onions finely. Fry them very slowly in a mixture of 2 tablespoons of oil and 3 of butter until translucent. Add red wine to generously cover the onions, boil for five minutes. Add one cup of grenadine syrup and one tablespoon of brown sugar, salt and pepper to taste and boil another ten minutes or

so. This will keep for months in the fridge.

Variations on this include:
Use honey instead of grenadine;
Use a mixture of good quality wine vinegar
and red wine, and one cup of brown sugar;
Substitute the sugar with red currant jelly;
Add two tablespoons of blackberry cordial
to any of the above.

Create your own personal confiture d'oignons,
bottle it in pretty pots, cover with circles of
a pretty fabric and delight your friends with
these much appreciated Christmas presents.

## Onion Soup

After a morning of cutting back brambles,
raking leaves, putting horse manure around the
rose bushes or hoeing around the broccoli plants,
it's the most satisfying thing to come in for a
lunch of steaming onion soup. Like most stews
and soups this tastes better on the second day.

### Onion Soup

Slice about 3 lbs. (1.35 kg) of onions finely and
sweat them in a combination of butter and oil.
They should be just on the point of getting black.
That's the moment to add 6 cups (1.2 litres)

of dry red wine and 2 chicken stock cubes.

Boil for 5 minutes. Add salt and pepper to taste. Toast one slice of bread per person. Sprinkle some grated cheese on each slice, pass under the grill for 2 minutes, place in a deep soup plate and pour the piping hot soup over it.

## Roasted Onions with Pine Kernels and Blue Cheese in Balsamic Vinegar Dressing

This is such a simple dish and so unbelievably good. You can make it ahead and warm it up just before serving.

Peel 4 large sweet onions, cut each of them into 8 sections, place into an oven-proof dish, sprinkle liberally with olive oil and roast at 350F (175°C) for about 1 to 1½ hours, turning them over three or four times. When they begin to get slightly charred, take the dish out of the oven. Cut up ¼ lb. (110g) of blue cheese (use a soft variety, Gorgonzola or Saint Agur), spread over the onions, add however many pine kernels you can afford (or substitute with walnuts), pour 1/3 of a cup of Balsamic vinegar over the whole thing, stir and serve lukewarm.
Serves 4 as a first course, 6 as a side dish.

## Baked Onions with Sausages

Prick 2 lbs. (900g) of breakfast sausages, place them into a rectangular oven-proof casserole. Slice 2 lbs. (900g) of sweet onions and put them on top of the sausages.

Sprinkle 1 teaspoon of salt and 1 teaspoon of freshly ground black pepper over them. Cover with 2½ cups (50 cl) of dry red wine and bake in a medium hot (350F, 175°C) oven for an hour. Baste occasionally and add more liquid if necessary.

Especially tasty on mashed potatoes to which you have added a cup (20 cl) of apple sauce.

## Hard-boiled Eggs in a Creamy Onion Sauce

Soak a few threads of saffron in ½ cup (10 cl) of lukewarm milk.

Hard boil 4 eggs, put them in cold water for ½ minute and peel them carefully. Keep warm.

Quarter 6 medium onions. Boil them slowly in 2 cups (40 cl) of milk to which you have added the saffron milk. When the onions are completely cooked, put them through a blender, adjust seasoning.

Put back into saucepan and warm the mixture to just up to boiling point. Add 3 tablespoons of thick cream, lower the eggs carefully into the mixture and serve on Basmati rice, accompanied by a green salad.

## Onion and Orange Salad with Fresh Mint (right)

Peel one orange per person. Cut into slices across the sections. Use the 3 middle slices and arrange on a plate. Skin a sweet onion and slice across, making onion rings. Place 2 or 3 onion rings on top of the orange slices. Fill the middle with

chopped fresh mint. Sprinkle with a dressing made of balsamic vinegar, olive oil and salt.

## Saffron Onions

In a saucepan, soak 1 teaspoon of saffron threads in ¾ cups (15 cl) each of wine vinegar, sunflower oil and water, 2 teaspoons of salt, 1 teaspoon of turmeric, 1 teaspoon of freshly ground black pepper and 2 teaspoons of sugar.

In the meantime fill a quart size (slightly less than one litre) Mason jar with finely sliced onions.

Let the saffron mixture come to a boil and quickly pour over the onions, seal, turn the jar upside down for a few minutes, then back to normal position. Repeat this a few times. It is ready as soon as it cools off, but can be kept for weeks. Once opened it should be kept in the fridge.

Delicious with cold boiled beef, cheese, ham etc.

You can substitute the saffron with harissa, the North African hot pepper sauce, or Tabasco.

Again, jars of this make a very welcome Christmas or house-warming gift.

# Figs

We have two fig trees, a huge one in the lower courtyard under whose deep shade we have lovely lunches in the summer. The other smaller one, which has even sweeter figs, has two trunks embedded in a stone wall which look exactly like elephant's feet.

From about the middle of August on, we can start picking this rich fruit. In a good year we probably get five thousand figs, at a conservative estimate. What to do with that many figs? Everybody with a garden has a fig tree here, so giving them away is not the answer. I have toyed with the idea of loading the car with four crates of slightly under-ripe figs, driving to Switzerland and selling them there. Too time consuming and not necessarily economically sound.

Every three years or so, nature asserts its right to confound our plans and the heavens open up just when the figs are at their best. Consequently they burst open, a gust of wind knocks them down and we have a carpet of fig purée, happily frequented by myriads of butterflies, wasps, flies and hornets…

Everyone in this region makes fig jam. I tried many of their recipes and always found the jam cloyingly sweet. Then I experimented. The best jam that I concocted is the following:

### Fig, Green Tomato and Walnut Jam

The green tomatoes add character and the walnuts make it really special. For every 3 cups of chopped figs, add 1 cup of chopped green tomatoes, ½ cup of chopped walnuts and 2½ cups (500g) of sugar.

Boil together rapidly until a dollop on a cold plate doesn't run any more.

### Caramelized Figs

Use small, green, very ripe figs for best results. In France, they are called figues blanches, white figs, to distinguish them from figues noires, purple figs.

In a skillet, melt 2 tablespoons of butter and a teaspoon of duck or goose fat for every 8 figs. Place the figs into the fat and warm them slowly, then turn the heat up slightly.

With a wooden spoon, shift the figs around frequently until they are almost black, about an hour to an hour and a half. They are so sweet that no sugar is needed. This makes a wonderful accompaniment to foie gras, magret de canard or pork roast.

**Another way of preparing caramelized figs is:**
Brush a dozen green figs with melted butter. Put them under the grill, but not too close. You have to be in the kitchen while you're doing this, surveying the process.

Turn them around every two minutes or so until they are brown.

They are delicious with grilled sausages or grilled bacon and make an unusual addition to a super Sunday brunch.

For a cocktail party or as a first course, wrap the figs in strips of any kind of raw, cured ham, Serrano, Aosta or jambon cru and secure with a tooth pick.

**Magret de Canard with Caramelized Figs**
Figure one magret for two people. Score the fat part in a criss-cross pattern and dredge with my Magic Spice. Leave at room temperature for a minimum of two hours.

When you are ready to cook, place them in a frying pan, fat side down, and heat them slowly.

When the fat begins to crackle turn around and increase the heat. Cover and cook for two or three minutes. Put them fat down again and let them reach the desired pinkness.

Here they are usually served a vivid pink, but personally I prefer them almost done. Slice them and arrange them prettily on a pre-warmed platter, accompanied by caramelized figs.

**Fig Meringue Pie**
Pre-bake a pie crust until about half done
Chop 3 cups of figs
Add 1 teaspoon of vanilla extract or lemon juice and 1½ egg yolks
Beat 3 egg whites with a pinch of salt until stiff
Add 2 tablespoons of icing sugar
Place the fig mixture onto the pastry shell, top with the meringue and bake in a pre-heated oven until the peaks of the meringue are almost black.

**Fig and Green Tomato Chutney**

2 lbs. (900g) of figs

2 cups of chopped, deseeded green tomatoes

2 sliced cloves of garlic

1 sliced onion

3 cups (60 cl) of cider vinegar

2 cups (350g) of brown sugar

Add ingredients and bring to a boil

Simmer for 4 minutes, and bottle in sterilised jars.

**Figs stuffed with Gorgonzola (*above*)**

The small figs are perfect for finger food; they are exactly a mouthful.

Cut a slice off the top. With the small end of an apple corer or a sharp grapefruit spoon, take out part of the inside of the fig and replace with Gorgonzola.

## Chicken Livers with Caramelized Figs on a Bed of Chicory

Start to caramelize the figs.
While they are getting shiny and brown, fry ¼ lb. (110g) of fresh chicken livers per person in butter until all the pink colour has disappeared. Keep warm.

For each serving, arrange two or three leaves of chicory (Belgian endive) on a plate. Place the warm chicken livers and the warm caramelized figs on top. Sprinkle with Balsamic vinegar and melted butter which you have whipped up with an egg whisk. Serve immediately.

*Peggy and Trilby enjoying the shade of the fig tree*

# Olives, Olives, Olives!

Mediterranean countryside
equals olive trees.
The very first things we
planted when we got to Les
Micocouliers were olive trees.
We wanted an olive grove.

I still have the bill from M. Caizergue, the nurseryman: 6 oliviers à ffrs 50= ffrs 300. He sure had us. Despite massive amounts of fertilizer, potash, multiple diggings, the advice of an olive tree "expert", the grafting by another olive tree man, we have yet to reap one single olive from those trees.

The three old, gnarled olive trees that were here when we bought the place have produced reasonably well though (*far right*).

In the first year we used the green olives and followed the recipe our neighbour gave us. We soaked them in soda for three weeks, rinsed them every day for another two, only to find that they weren't very good. Now I let them get ripe, beautifully black. At Christmas it has become a ritual for the whole family to pick the shiny ebony fruit, invariably in warm sunshine. I prepare them in the following old-fashioned way:

### Preserving Olives

Prick each olive three times with a fork. Place in a large, wide bowl.

For every 5 pounds (about 2.2 kg) of olives, use a cup of coarse sea salt, and mix it with the olives.

Three times a day, every day for 5 weeks, shake them carefully. At the end of that time taste them. There should be no bitterness left.

Place in jars with tight-fitting lids made of cork or glass, add 1/3 cup (7 cl) of olive oil, spices to suit your preference (garlic, lemon rind, summer savoury, thyme...), cover and leave for another two weeks before eating.

We usually leave the olives at the top of the trees to the birds and I keep a basketful in the courtyard. I run my hands through them when I pass: better than hand cream!

Wild thyme

*Our own olives with lemon rind, garlic and thyme*

# Zucchini

There is a moment every summer, when you cannot even *give* away zucchini. One day you have tiny little yellow or green zucchini and you think it would be a shame to pick them at that stage, and the next day they are huge.

And they keep producing and getting big.
You make stir fried zucchini. You make zucchini au gratin.
You make stuffed zucchini.
You make zucchini soup and you make zucchini bread.
And then you simply cannot look at another zucchini or envisage processing one in any way whatsoever.
Still, I have a few recipes that might stimulate even the most fed-up zucchini eaters.

**Yellow and Green Zucchini Patties**
2 x 12 inch (30 cm) green zucchini (the darker green the better!)
2 x 12 inch yellow zucchini
3 x tablespoons of buckwheat flour
3 tablespoons of fine polenta
4 tablespoons of chopped parsley
1 teaspoon of green food colouring
1 teaspoon of turmeric
2 eggs
Salt and pepper

4 tablespoons of corn oil
4 tablespoons of butter

Grate the zucchini, putting the green ones in one bowl and the yellow ones in another.

To the green ones add: the buckwheat flour, the parsley, the green food colouring and one egg.

Mix the yellow zucchini with the yellow corn flour, the turmeric and the other egg. Season. Heat the butter and the oil in a large skillet and fry the zucchini mixture by dropping large spoonfuls into the fat. Flatten them slightly with a spatula. Fry them about three or four minutes on each side. Don't let them get black.

Serve with Daniel's Hot Salsa (page 76) and a green salad.

### Zucchini or Pumpkin Bread

Beat four eggs and 1½ cups (270g) of brown sugar until frothy. Add 1¼ cups (25 cl) of vegetable oil, 1 cup (115g) of ordinary flour, 1 cup (115g) of whole wheat flour and 1 cup (115g) of a mixture of fine corn meal, buckwheat flour and oat germ, plus 1 teaspoon of salt, 2 teaspoons of baking soda and 2 teaspoons of pumpkin pie spice. Stir in 3 cups of grated, unpeeled zucchini.

Pour into 2 buttered and floured rectangular cake pans and place in a COLD oven. Set temperature at 320F (160°C). Bake the bread for at least 50 minutes or until a toothpick that you stick into the dough comes out clean. Let cool in the pans.

This freezes very well and is much appreciated by young and old. It may well be that my grandchildren, when they are old, will associate zucchini bread more than anything else with their holidays at Les Micocouliers.

You can substitute the zucchini with pumpkin. The method is the same.

# Goat Cheese

We get the most delicious goat cheeses here. Their local name is "pélardons" and they play a big role in the Cévenole cuisine.

They are at their best during May and June when the goats feast on the fresh grass.
Which reminds me of a story: Goats are known for their voracity. They'll try everything once. When two of these animals picked over a rubbish tip, one of them nibbled on a film reel. The other one looked at him aghast and said: is that good? Whereupon the first goat replied: not as good as the book !
But back to pélardons.
Every restaurant in the region features a first course of grilled pélardons on a bed of salad. No cheese platter would be complete without at least 3 types of goat cheese in various stages of ripeness.
Fresh, or semi-fresh, creamy goat cheese lends itself to many appetizing mousses and canapé spreads and dips. I haven't found a satisfactory way of using the strong-tasting hard ones. The difficulty in compiling recipes is that these cheeses are not factory made. They vary literally from producer to producer, from day to day and from season to season, depending on the weather, the temperature, the food the goats are feeding on, and how you store them.
I can therefore only give approximate quantities. You will have to experiment and add more or less liquid, salt, olive oil or even maybe a little blue cheese, if the goat cheese is bland. On the whole I find that the pepper family has an affinity with goat cheese, be it roast red peppers or diverse ground peppercorns, black, white red and green.

**Goat Cheese Spread**
For a lovely spread, either on crackers, toast or in celery stalks, try this:
    With each goat cheese of about 2 oz. (60g) use 3 tablespoons of liquid cream, one teaspoon of chopped chives, one teaspoon of my Magic Spice (page 119), a strip of roast pepper, about 1 by 2 inches (2 ½ by 5 cm), a soupçon of chopped

garlic and a tablespoon of walnut oil. Put in blender until smooth. Don't add salt before tasting. Some goat cheeses are quite salty.

### Sliced Tomato and Goat Cheese Salad
Arrange slices of firm tomatoes on a platter. Chop some pélardons and spread them on top. Sprinkle minced fresh basil over them and drench with my favourite salad dressing (page 117).

When I write the word cuisine I think of the time I tried to find a cook book called Cuisine of the Sun. I went to Brentano's in New York and asked one of the salespeople to help me find it. She got the big reference book out, but wasn't getting anywhere. When I asked to have a look at it myself I realized that she had been looking under Q....

# Les MUSTS at Les Micocouliers

Our life at Les Micocouliers is quiet for most of the year. But there is an invasion of family members and friends beginning in late June, and continuing until well into September.

Since we are able to sleep up to twenty two people at one time, not including those in tent arrangements in the garden, it sometimes feels more like a hotel than a private dwelling. This area has so much to offer in terms of sightseeing (diverse grottes, menhirs, cascades, spectacular canyons etc.), sports activities, beaches and picnics, berry picking and mushrooming, that guests are never at a loss for something to do.

In the winter, a smaller version of this invasion takes place around Christmas time.

No summer season would be complete without at least one canoe trip from La Foux to Navacelles. Let me explain:

The Vis is a river that joins the Hérault river just above Ganges. Upriver from that spot it is visible for only about fifteen kilometres. Beyond that it runs underground and surges out into the open at a place called La Foux (pronounced foox). The force with which it bursts out of the rocks gave people the excellent idea of building a water mill there. I don't know how old the mill is, but it hasn't been in use since before World War II. One wheel is covered in moss, as there is no longer a roof on the mill. After a good rain, water gushes out from every old window and every crevice. It's a spectacular sight!

La Foux

This is where our stalwarts lower the canoes into the water which is extremely cold, even in the heat of August. The trip then takes them through a wild and inaccessible five kilometres to the little village of Navacelles. Water snakes and lots of kingfishers are always sighted. At the little bridge near Navacelles, someone not quite up to the canoe trip will be waiting with a bunch of Chrish's special Foux Sandwiches, as they have come to be known.

**Chrish's Foux Sandwiches (right)**
The day before the outing, Chrish buys one "gros pain" (same as a baguette, but bigger) for every three persons. If the bread is too fresh, it won't absorb the filling as well. Early the following morning, she cuts them open lengthwise, dribbles olive oil over them and rubs fresh garlic on the inside.

Then she spreads sliced sweet onions, hard boiled eggs, canned tuna, sliced tomatoes, pitted black olives, salt, pepper, harissa (the Tunisian hot pepper paste) and lettuce on them. If there are any good leftovers from the previous day, they can also be popped into the sandwiches. When all this has been nicely distributed, the two halves of the bread are carefully put back together, wrapped in aluminium foil and placed on the marble coffee table. Chrish then covers them with wooden boards and weighs these down with heavy stones or another slab of marble. After a couple of hours she cuts them into individual portions and wraps them up again in foil or saran wrap.

They always taste fabulous, and the olive oil should be trickling down the corners of your mouth as you eat. When you have just come through the Gorge of the Vis river, having probably fallen once or twice into the frigid water, they are like Manna from Heaven.

## Another MUST is Egyptian Night

Not to be missed at any cost! Even though we serve any number of Middle Eastern delicacies at this summer feast, it is always known as Egyptian night. Perhaps because we all get dressed in Egyptian djellabas, head scarves with dangling coins and other accoutrements.

The tape player gets loaded with Arabic music, especially the singing of the legendary Om Kalthoum, and some courageous woman occasionally makes a stab at a belly dance to the frenetic accompaniment of ululations from the crowd. I often wonder what our staid French neighbours think when they hear all this, but so far no gendarmes have ever shown up.

For me, Egypt's culinary highlight is stuffed pigeons, but I have never tried my hand at them. Pigeons are not easy to find and I know I couldn't do justice to them. Our friend Mahmoud Makhlouf from Cairo had a cook who turned out real marvels, usually stuffed with bulgur wheat and delicately flavoured with wonderful spices.

Couscous is actually more of a Maghreb (Tunisia, Algeria and Morocco) dish, but that is what we have, huge mounds of it. And not the quick stuff I make (see under quick couscous, page 40), but the real thing.

Here follows a couscous recipe, originally gleaned from Chrish's Algerian friend Chérifa, but then also influenced by her Moroccan cook

Fatima as well as her Tunisian friend Raja.
It is essential to have seven vegetables for a
decent couscous.
Choose among the following: red and green
peppers, eggplant, cardoon, carrots, fennel,
pumpkin, leeks, zucchini, broad beans, cabbage,
potatoes, chick peas, turnips.

### Couscous à l'Agneau
2½ lbs. (a generous kilo) lamb, leg or shoulder,
cut up into 2 inch pieces
1 cup olive oil
2 medium onions
4 tbls. tomato paste
1½ tbls. sweet dried red pepper (paprika)
2 tbls. ras el hanout (couscous spice, available
in most specialty shops, or make your own
with cumin, red pepper, turmeric, saffron,
black pepper)

1 tsp. dried hot pepper or harissa
2 cloves of garlic
Salt and pepper
3 zucchini
1 green cabbage, preferably the curly kind
3 cups of pumpkin, cut into large chunks
3-4 carrots, whole
3-4 baby turnips, whole
2-3 pieces of cardoon
2 green and one red pepper
2 cups of chick peas, soaked in water overnight,
then cooked separately with 1 teaspoon of salt
until tender
3 cups of couscous grain, preferably imported
Cap Bon

Sauté the onions until golden, add the meat
and the ras el hanout, the sweet pepper powder
and a cup or two of water so the meat can absorb
the spices. Add the tomato paste, salt and pepper
and stir well. Simmer over medium heat. When
the meat is about half done, add the cleaned
vegetables and the cooked chick peas.
Cover and continue to cook, stirring from time to
time. If the vegetables seem done before the
meat, remove them and continue cooking
until the meat is done and add vegetables
at the very end. They must not be mushy.
You can make a separate hot
sauce from the stock of this
mixture, adding some harissa or
other hot red pepper sauce.
Prepare the couscous according
to package directions, or if you are
lucky enough to get the real thing,
make it in the traditional way.
On a large platter, arrange the

couscous grain and sprinkle with some of the sauce from the meat and vegetable mixture. Pile the chickpeas on top and add the vegetables and meat, creating a kind of attractive pyramid. Serve the rest of the sauce and the hot sauce separately.

For those who like it even hotter, you can fry small green peppers in oil (deseed them first !) and pass around with the couscous.

This should serve six to eight people. As a starter we serve Baba Ghanouj or Hommos with sliced carrots and cucumbers.

### Cucumber and Yoghurt Salad

Peel, deseed and grate two or three fine cucumbers. Add a teaspoon of rock salt and let stand for a few minutes. Drain and add yoghurt, finely chopped garlic, chopped fresh mint and ground black pepper.

My son J-B and Jim on the Vis.

I am afraid that even the desserts have nothing at all to do with Egypt: theirs are too much work, too sweet and too heavy. Instead we make a dessert of sliced oranges (page 122) or a pretty fruit salad, to bring the feast to a healthy end.

### River Picnics on the Vis

A crusty Cévenol fellow called André used to be our gardener and handyman. He has now retired but still comes to plant our onions each spring. He has a wonderful and secluded piece of property on the Vis river, a tributary to the Hérault, where we have a fantastic cook-out every year.

André has built a sort of oven with native stones. He makes a roaring fire in it and when the embers are good and hot, places what he calls "un diable", literally a devil, inside. This diable is shaped like a huge acorn, pointed at the bottom and made out of terracotta. That is where the whole potatoes, freshly picked from his garden and washed in the river, go.

He throws in a bunch of local herbs, summer savoury, fennel and thyme, adds a bit of olive oil and some rock salt, puts the lid on and lets them cook. In the meantime he catches a couple of huge trout from his fish basin. These he grills over a cedar fire and brushes them with rosemary twigs dipped in olive oil.

All this is accompanied by tomatoes just off the vine - and of course copious amounts of vin du pays, the delicious local rosé or red wine.

While all the cooking is going on, the younger generation go out on the river in canoes and inflatable tires and have a great old time throwing each other into the water or sunbathing on the rocks.

## Ammoniting

You won't find the verb *to ammonite* in the dictionary. We coined it, in our family, meaning to go and look for ammonites, those pretty petrified snails which occur in abundance just a couple of miles from Les Micocouliers.
And it is such fun!

The best time to go is during the Christmas holidays, when the low sun throws its rays across the slight ribbing of the ammonites, thus making them more easily detectable. In the summer, when the sun is high, it is much harder to spot them.

We usually go with all the children, spreading out across the hill, until someone shouts: "Good one! Come and look!"

We all rush to admire the fossil and then start to look for more in the same space, as they have a tendency to occur in groups. It is easy to forget the time, until hunger pangs remind us to go home and partake of some kind of delicious body-and-soul-warming soup.

As an example our friend Daniel's hearty oxtail soup:

### Daniel's Oxtail Soup

Cut an oxtail into pieces and brown these in a mixture of vegetable oil and butter for about 15 minutes, turning them all the while.

Place them in a stew pot, cover with 6 cups (1.2 litres) of water, add a sliced onion, 2 cubed carrots, a branch of celery, a bay leaf, ½ a teaspoon of thyme, some parsley stalks, a beef cube, salt and pepper plus half a cup of pearl barley. Cook slowly for about three hours.

Now remove all the vegetables and discard them. Sweat a chopped onion and a grated carrot in butter. Cool the broth, take the meat off the bones and remove the fat. Add the carrots, onion and meat to the soup and reheat.

J-B, our son, used to bring lots of his friends (*below*) down from Cambridge to help around the house. They would even climb onto the scaffolding and hack away at the old "crépis" to reveal the beautiful stonework underneath. They were at an age when they literally inhaled their food. Three or even four of John's famous cheese sandwiches each was the norm, accompanied by home made sweet pickles (page 62) and saffron onions (page 86). I won't mention how much vin du pays went down their gullets on these occasions.

### John's Cheese Sandwiches

He must have prepared hundreds of them. Whether it was just one for himself or twenty for family and guests, he produced the most delicious and deservedly famous cheese sandwiches. He used Cantal Entre-Deux cheese, similar to Cheddar, with just that little tang to it. For bread he used the sliced wholemeal type. There was one he particularly liked and that whoever came down here from England had to bring, Allinson's dark brown loaf.

Everybody got to choose between mayonnaise and butter, onion, no onion, harissa, no harissa, a slice of tomato or not.

His own favourite was mayo, cheese, four thin slices of onion and harissa. He then put the sandwiches under the grill until the cheese melted and the onions turned brown.

# Beloved Blackberries

**Every other year or so, around mid August and into September, we get an abundance of wild blackberries**

Much as we hate the thorny bushes and deep roots in the garden, when they produce juicy berries in the endless hedges we gather them with great pleasure The luscious, shiny fruit are a wonderful anti-oxidant and I use them in many different recipes. Picked fresh they add health and flavour to Muesli and breakfast cereal. Mixed with yoghurt and a little sugar, honey or a spoonful of apricot jam, they make a yummy snack. They freeze extremely well and can be added year round to fruit salad or Mock Pavlova (page 34).

Add some to your apple crumble for a different and delicious version.

**Blackberry Jam**

I make a seedless jam, half way between a regular jam and jelly, the following way:

Place 2½ lbs. (1.35 kg) of blackberries in a saucepan, cover with water and boil for 10 minutes.

Pass through the finest blade of a food mill (a must, available in Europe or speciality shops) Measure the liquid.

For each cup (20 cl) of juice, use ¾ of a cup (150g) of sugar. Boil until it sets. Pour into sterilized jars and screw the tops on tightly.

Turn upside down for 2 minutes, then right side up. Repeat two or three times. You will hear the pop of the creation of the vacuum, which means that the jam is sterilized.

**Blackberry and Apple Crumble**

Place frozen or fresh blackberries on the bottom of an oven-proof dish. Add peeled, sliced apples, ½ teaspoon of cinnamon or 2 teaspoons of lemon juice. Cover with basic crumble mix:

## Basic Crumble Mix

2 cups (250g) flour

1 cup (125g) sugar

4 ½ oz. (114g) chilled butter

Process in blender or food processor for one minute.

Bake in a moderate oven until it smells delicious and the fruit is bubbling.

For a different crumble mix try this:

¾ cups (200g) buckwheat flour

2 oz (50g) of ground almonds

or hazelnuts (*left*)

1 cup (110g) sugar

# Wild Mushrooms

Gathering wild mushrooms is for me one of the most enjoyable pastimes imaginable. I am not alone. Judging from the amount of mushroom books sold, the increasing number of web sites on mycology and the people one meets on all the forays and mycological exhibitions, this hobby is fast becoming extremely popular.

Fortunately for me, most of the mushroomers around here are interested in only a few varieties, cèpes (porcini), chanterelles, maybe Horn of Plenty and the Hedgehog Fungus.

I started to seriously identify fungi in Switzerland, where every town has a Pilzkontrolleur, a certified mycological expert, to whom you can bring your specimens and who will identify the mushrooms for you. When I was able to definitely recognize thirteen varieties I was thrilled. I went on forays, attended mycological seminars and bought books.

Tricholoma terreum

When we moved to the Cévennes I was in mushroom heaven. This is such a happy combination of habitats; I often come home with fifteen or even twenty types of edible mushrooms. Within at most one hour's drive we have forests of pine, beech, Holm oak and chestnut trees, each representing a different mycological habitat and therefore a varied harvest.

I have even collected kilos of precious chanterelles in my own garden.

The most popular of all the mushrooms is undoubtedly the cèpe (porcini in Italian). In my opinion its taste is vastly overrated except in its dried state and I know scores of varieties with a much better flavour, but the joy of finding a healthy, splendid boletus edulis, to give it its Latin name, is indescribable.

In this area many of my mushrooming friends manage to come home with ten kilos (22 lbs.) or more of these treasures. I personally have never been that lucky, but I think it's because my eyes wander to every little protuberance and go more for variety than quantity.

Here is what I brought home on a typical day:

## Edible Mushrooms, October 5, 2005

Boletus edulis
Xerocomus badius
Suillus grevillei
Suillus luteus
Suillus granulatus
Suillus aeruginascens
Lycoperdon perlatum
Lycoperdon umbrinum
Sparassis crispa
Cantharellus lutescens
Laccaria laccata
Laccaria laccata, var. amethystina
Amanita vaginata
Gomphidius glutinosus
Tricholoma terreum
Hypholoma capnoides
Macrolepiota procera
Melanoleuca melaleuca
Russula mustelina
Russula integra
Russula coerulia
Russula puellaris
Russula amethystina

*Gomphidius glutinosus*

I try not to wash the mushrooms.
With a paper towel and a soft brush I clean
them and sort them into three categories.
Cook right away; eat or freeze
Dry in my mushroom drier
Pickle

In order to get the best flavour, I like to mix
the fresh mushrooms of the very best-
tasting varieties (russulas, amanita vaginata,
gomphidius glutinosus, suillus granulatus,
tricholoma terreum).

### Mushroom Ragoût

I chop half a large onion and let it soften in a bit
of butter and oil, add a small clove of minced
garlic and the mushrooms, cut into bite sized
pieces. Within just a couple of minutes the most
wonderful odor starts to emanate from the pan.
It doesn't take long for the mixture to be ready. If
we don't eat it right away, I freeze it for later use.

To serve, I add half a cup of cream, reheat
it and use it on pasta, with risotto, on toast, in
vols-au-vent or on freshly home-made mashed
potatoes, known in our family as mush-'n-mash.

Of course there are other ways of dealing with
the bounty from woods and fields. I pick many
types of excellent driers (older cèpes, xerocomus
badius, both types of laccaria laccata, the older
specimens of amanita vaginata, cantharelli etc).
To that end I have bought two mushroom
dryers in Switzerland. They consist of a heating
element at the bottom, with four to six or even
eight metal sieves placed over it. I cut larger
mushrooms into slices, leave smaller ones whole
and spread them on the many sieves of the
dryer. They are usually dry by the next morning.
This method provides probably the most
versatility. After soaking the dried mushrooms

*Dried cèpes*

am lucky, I find some chroogomphus helveticus or rutilus. It is in itself not very interesting on the culinary front, but it has the distinction of turning violet when cooked, thus giving the pickle mixture added beauty.

### Pickled Mushrooms

I let them all come to a boil in salted water, drain them and boil them again for one minute in white wine vinegar, to which I add salt and herbs. I then decant them into mason jars or glass jars with a plastic top, dribble a bit of olive oil over them and seal them. They keep for at least a year.

Pickled mushrooms are best served to accompany cold cuts and pâtés, in mixed salads, with cheese raclette or with a cheese board. They look very pretty and give any hors d'oeuvre dish an interesting note.

in warm water or wine, use them in any kind of stew, in sauces, in soup, mixed into the potatoes for Pommes Dauphinoises, cooked in béchamel sauce and put into patty shells, in risotto dishes, on toast and in omelets or scrambled eggs. If you don't use the liquid in which you have soaked the mushrooms, strain it through a very fine sieve or a piece of butter muslin, reduce and add to mashed potatoes, risotto or soup - a treat!

Dried mushrooms can be ground into mushroom powder, a very useful condiment for omelettes, fried eggs, soups, marinades, batter for Wienerschnitzel, etc.

### Pickling Mushrooms

For pickling I choose small tricholoma terreum, capnoides, cantharellus, some laccaria laccata, some of the suillus types, if they are firm, and poplar mushrooms (agrocybe aegerita). When I

The lepiota procera, or parasol mushroom, as it is called here because of its large hat, up to one foot across, dries beautifully. However it is so good freshly fried in butter, like a veal escalope, that I rarely end up with many of them in my dried mushroom provisions.

Very late in the season, in November and December, we are sometimes lucky and find the Horn of Plenty. Its sinister looks have caused it to be called trompette de la mort in French, and in German *Todestrompeten*, death trumpet. Despite its look and sinister name, this is a superb mushroom, very sought after in most parts of Europe. Sautéed for a few minutes in butter and served with cream, it is the most delicious topping for pasta.

It dries very well, but unfortunately turns bitter

when frozen.

Indeed, I'm quite bitten by the mushroom bug. I have mushroom shaped candles, all sorts of dishes with mushroom motifs, old etchings, new paintings, and my husband even etched some lovely mushroom shapes into the glass panes of the front door.

I have mushroom books in many languages, some very old ones, dating from the beginning of the 19th century. It is a pleasure to browse through them and see how the names, the edibility and the abundance of many mushrooms have changed in the last two hundred years. Some, like the tricholoma equestris, one of the most popular market mushrooms in Germany and widely esteemed

Lepista nudum
(blewit)

everywhere, has just recently been designated fungus non gratus after apparently causing several deaths in the Bordeaux region.

I think the main thing is moderation. Don't eat wild mushrooms every day of the week. With that warning in mind, enjoy these treasures from the wild as a delicious once in a while treat.

As you can imagine, my favourite time of the year is the fall, with its profusion of wild mushrooms, some late gentians and arnica, cool nights, figs and grapes – and unfortunately, hunting.

For sure there are too many boar around and they do much damage in olive groves, in vineyards, even in gardens, where they dig up flower bulbs, tulips being their favourites. They eat cherries off the trees and on our dog walks we see the evidence in their droppings.

But the woods are dangerous in the hunting season. I never venture forth without inquiring where there is a *battue*, which uses many dogs and hunters, and since I don't have much confidence in the latter's shooting prowess, I avoid them like the plague. There is never a season without one or more fatal shootings. The biggest day for the hunters is Sunday, so Sunday we stay put.

The rest of the week I'll go mushrooming at the drop of a hat, often accompanied by my favourite mushrooming friends Laure or Dominique. There are no excuses to hold me back. Washing, ironing, gardening, cleaning, all can wait. It's the best fun, wandering around the forest and admiring flora and fauna, and on top of that finding little jewels here and there.

Laccaria laccata, var. amethystina

# Christmas

The ceiling in our music room is very high which makes it possible to put up a 5 metre tree. We used to get it from the forester, freshly cut, and he would bring it in his special truck, warning lights blazing, very exciting.

Sometimes he would even let our men (son, sons-in-law and grandsons), go with him to pick the tree and help cut it down. The smell was fantastic and it was so much safer to have the tree fresh, because we use real candles. Unfortunately he isn't allowed to sell trees any more.

When my children were, well, children, we used to spend Christmas and the winter months in Davos, Switzerland. Although we were stationed in Tunisia, Paris or London, I managed to enter them into the Swiss kindergarten and school system in Davos. There were so many advantages: they learned Swiss and High German and were able to ski all winter. They acquired those quaint art skills, prevalent on the continent, such as making their own Christmas cards, cutting out Scherenschnitt, making little fairy walnut beds; the girls learned to knit and crochet and to do cross stitch embroidery; we all gilded dried flowers and pine cones. They were later able to impart all these arts to their own children and grandchildren.

**Christmas Cards**
Cut thin black cardboard into the required size. Draw Christmas motives and write wishes on them with a gold pen. Split straws in half and fashion stars or angels with them, then glue them onto the cards.

**Walnut Fairy Beds**
For little fairy beds split a walnut in half, remove the insides, then line the half shell with a little cotton. Make a tiny duvet with a piece of cloth, place a little manikin inside (draw a face on a wooden bead), drill a hole on each side of the "cradle", pass thin string through and hang this original ornament on the Christmas tree.

We also spent long evenings cutting out elaborate Scherenschnitt, using green and red tissue paper, which we folded multiple times and then cut out hearts and other charming shapes. These we would then glue onto window panes. Looking into a candle-lit room through these lacy creations gives a wonderfully festive, Christmassy feeling.

To decorate the table for the Christmas Eve dinner, we came up with new ideas every year:

*Santa Claus appears inside a peanut*

Christmas preparations is baking, and Linzertorte is one of the crucial items. I make it every year now and the entire family looks forward to it. I should mention at this juncture that my cake-making career did not get off to a very auspicious start. John and I were married in September and he got his first job as a geologist in Denver, Colorado. After an initial stay in the little house in Golden, Colorado, just outside Denver, we moved to the Mount Vernon Country Club area, 900 feet above Golden.

A tangerine with a candle stuck in it for every person; a centrepiece of two gilded pineapples, also with candles in them; golden seashells, empty snail houses, peanuts and walnuts, or even just pretty pebbles strewn at random around pine boughs; pomegranates with silver stars glued on them; three or four different types of pine cones, tied together with a string and attached to the old oil lamp dangling above the table.

As the years passed I was able to watch the wonderment on the faces of first my children, then my grandchildren, and now my great-grandchildren, as they were initiated into the miracle of a Santa Claus head appearing inside a split peanut kernel! (*page 113*)

However, the most important item in our

John's birthday came in January and I was determined to bake him a birthday cake. Desserts have never been my thing, but I thought I did know how to make an ordinary basic Madeira cake with butter, sugar, eggs, vanilla extract and flour.

What nobody had told me was that mile high baking is different from sea-level baking. I can't remember what you have to change; I only know that the cake came out of the oven a complete flop. Fortunately John kept to himself what he thought about having such an incompetent wife…

But what really killed my desire to ever want to bake a cake again was that shortly after the above fiasco, John decided to show me how to bake a cake. He mixed and stirred and poured the batter into a cake form, and bingo, into the preheated oven – oh, oh! He had forgotten to put the sugar in! Out came the cake, out came the batter, sugar incorporated, back into the oven – and the cake came out *perfectly*.

That put such a damper on me that I didn't bake anything again until we were back in Europe and I mastered the complicated Linzertorte, a latticed, jam-filled cake that I traditionally now make for Christmas as well as Easter.

It freezes beautifully and everyone in the family – including the in-laws, grandchildren and great-grandchildren – loves it.

### Linzertorte

For 2 rectangular Linzertortes, about 9" by 12" (22 by 28 cm) each

14 oz. (400g) unsalted butter
1¾ cups (400g) sugar
4 medium eggs
Pinch of salt
Grated zest of 1 lemon
2 teaspoons pumpkin pie spice
14 oz. (400g) ground hazelnuts
About 6½ cups (750g) flour
1 teaspoon baking powder
10 oz. (300g) red currant jam
10 oz. (300g) raspberry jam
1 beaten egg yolk for brushing
the top of the pastry

Soften the butter over warm water or in a warming oven. Do *not completely melt it.* Meanwhile, grind the hazelnuts and put aside. When the butter is soft, add the sugar, the eggs, salt, spice, zest and hazelnuts, beating vigorously after each ingredient. Add the sifted flour and baking powder. The dough has to be able to keep its shape, but should not be dry. Butter and flour the cake pans. (I like to use Pyrex glass dishes).

Now grab a handful of dough (less than half of it) and start patting it into the dish with the back of your hand which you have previously dipped in flour.

The dough will stick to your hand, so keep dipping it into the flour. The bottom of the cake should be about ¼ inch (5 mm) thick. Then form the sides by pushing the dough with the back of your hand up against the rim. Make it about ¾ inch (1.8 cm) high and just under ¼ inch (4 mm) wide. Take your time to make everything even. Dip a dinner fork into the flour; make dents into the top of the rim, all around. Preheat the oven to 350F (175°C). Mix the two types of jam together and spread evenly on the cake bottom.

On a floured board roll out some of the Linzertorte dough into a rectangular shape about 1/10 inch (2.5 mm) thick. With a fluted pastry wheel, cut strips the length of the cake form. Transfer carefully, with the help of a long flat knife or spatula, on top of the jam, one third from each end, in other words, two strips at an equal distance. Re-spread the dough, cut strips the *width* of the cake dish. Place the first one in the centre, then one on each side.

Separate an egg, add 1 tsp. of water to the yolk and with a pastry brush apply very carefully on top of the rim and on top of the strips.

Bake about 40 minutes at 350F (175°C), or until it smells done.

Repeat for the second one!

## Mailänderli

The second most important thing we bake at Christmas is Mailänderli cookies. I wonder why they are called Mailänderli. Mailand is German for Milan and I don't think these delicious cookies come from there. It's the perfect Christmas thing.

When still hot, you pierce them with a thin knitting needle to make a hole. Once they are cold you pull a thread through the hole and hang them on the Christmas tree.

There are so many shapes you can do, animals, letters of the alphabet etc, but my favourites are stars and Christmas trees.

When my grandchildren from Egypt used to come for Christmas, I hung them from the ceiling for the upper bunk and through the slats of the upper bunk for the lower bunk. That way they could just pluck the goodies above their heads and munch them.

### Mailänderli
9 oz (250g) unsalted butter
1 cup (220g) of sugar
1 egg and 2 egg yolks
Grated zest of 1 lemon

Pinch of salt
4¼ cups
(500g) of
flour
1 egg yolk
for the glaze

Soften the
butter (do *not* melt it),
beat the sugar and the eggs
into it. Add the grated lemon zest. Sieve the flour
and salt into the mixture. Form into a ball, cover
in grease-proof paper and let rest in the fridge for
at least an hour.

Take the dough out and let it reach room
temperature before rolling it out on a floured
board and cutting out the different shapes.
Brush with egg yolk and bake in medium heat
until golden. The time depends on how thick you
make them and that is a matter of preference.

And of course no Christmas Eve is complete
without a Zopf (literally a braid or tresse).

## Zopf

This is not going to be easy, since:
*a.* I never measure anything when I make it
*b.* You're supposed to use a special Zopf flour
which you can buy in many Swiss grocery stores,
including the famous Migros stores.
I have made it in many different places with
ordinary flour. It just doesn't hold its shape
as well.
So here goes:

### Zopf

Soften ¼ of a lb. (110g) of butter (by cutting
into pieces and putting in a little bowl above
some hot water, it must not get liquid!).

In a big bowl dissolve 1 oz (30g) of fresh
yeast in a cup (20 cl) of half milk, half warm
water, add 1 teaspoon of sugar, 3 tablespoons
of flour, stir, cover and leave for about 20
minutes. The mixture should get frothy.

Stir in the softened butter, a whole egg and
2 scant teaspoons of salt. Then add 1¾ lbs.
(800g) of flour and about a cup (20 cl) of half

milk and half warm water (maybe more), a little of each at a time. This is where I simply don't know for sure how much. At the end you should have a ball of dough that is elastic.

Cover it and let it rise in a warm place for about 1½ to 2 hours (or alternatively overnight in the fridge. That works quite well !)

Take it out unto a floured board, knead and knock and slap it for 10 minutes. If it's sticky, add more flour. Now comes the really tricky part: cut the dough in half and form 2 snakes about 15 inches (37 cm) long and 1½ inches (4 cm) thick. This takes quite a lot of time; you have to roll it with the palm of one hand and stretch it with the other hand.

To form the "braid" lay one snake of dough horizontally (A), the other one at a right angle on top (B).

With your right hand pull the left half of snake A across B, with your left hand the right half of A across B.

Then with your right hand pull the upper half of B down and slightly to the right, the lower half of B up to the left.

Repeat until you have nothing left. Squeeze the four ends together. It should now look like a braid.

Put on baking sheet and let rise another ½ hour. Stir an egg yolk with a couple of drops of cold water and brush it on the Zopf. Leave for 20 minutes in the cold.

Heat the oven to 350F (175 °C), bake for about 50 minutes or until it smells right. Thump the bottom of the Zopf with your knuckles. It should sound slightly hollow.

During the second world war all the ingredients for Zopf were rationed, flour, butter, eggs, milk, so we didn't get to taste it for a long time, but one Christmas my mother decided to save up the top of the milk (not pasteurized then!), and enough flour, butter and an egg to make a Zopf. It all went swimmingly; the oven was lit and in went the Zopf – only to be entirely forgotten by us all until the dreadful smell of burning had us rush into the kitchen. Too late, there was not even a morsel that tasted okay.

A similar thing happened to a friend of mine here in France. When her husband brought home the first fresh cèpes mushrooms of the season, always an event, she cooked them up with garlic and parsley, only instead of olive oil, she added dish washing liquid….

# Memorable Parties and Cakes

No matter where we happened to be living on New Year's Eve, we always managed to get some good parties going.

There must be hundreds of people who over the years have been guests and part of our celebrations. Three things were de rigueur:
– Playing charades
– Baking a whole ham and decorating it with a slalom ski run
– Potato Salad (page 80)

## Charades

There have been some unbelievably funny moments, like the time a whole team was supposed to guess "dollar". They got as far as "American" and "money", but not one of them came up with dollar, while the opposite team was rolling on the floor with laughter.

Or the time an admiral of the British Navy tried to get the word "torpedo" across to his team. He was wagging his hand behind his bottom and charging around the room, and all his side could come up with was "tail", "bush", and much worse – to the amusement of the competition.

The children and grandchildren and now the great-grandchildren were introduced early to this fun game. They would start out by imitating one of our many cats washing its paws, or when the clue was "ice cream", doing a good job of licking an imaginary ice cream cone.

## Ham

It was sometimes not easy to get a raw, whole, smoked ham, but with a bit of perseverance we always prevailed.

This is how John made it:

### John's Ham

Place a 13 lb. (5 kg) raw, smoked ham into a large stew pot the day before. Cover with water.

Next day, pour the water off, cover it with fresh water. Add an onion, studded with cloves, and a handful of black peppercorns.

Let it come to a boil, then reduce the heat and keep it simmering for 3 hours.

Take it out, remove the rind and score it criss-cross with a knife. At each crossing, place a clove.

Baste with a honey and mustard sauce and bake in a medium oven for 45 minutes.

To decorate create a ski slope with icing sugar and position little flags (toothpicks with bits of paper) to simulate a slalom run. At the top place a sign with "START", at the bottom one with "ZIEL". We have a wooden skier that gets stuck somewhere between the "gates".

Another custom on New Year's Eve has become the ringing out of the Old Year and ringing in of the New. This we do with a lovely bell that Bob Baird, who used to be my son's house master at Eton, brought us as a house warming gift. He came by train and carried the heavy cast iron beauty in his rucksack. He had it specially cast and our name engraved on it. We all assemble on the balcony at about five minutes to midnight. At one minute to, the specially designated person tolls the bell, stops at midnight, then rings in the New Year among lusty singing of Auld Lang Syne, fireworks and champagne.

However, undoubtedly the most memorable New Year's party took place on the 31st of

*Bob's bell*

December, 1981.

Our youngest daughter, Andrea, got married that day! All the red tape involved when a Swiss citizen and a British subject decide to get married in France was successfully taken care of. The civil ceremony took place in the old "mairie", performed by Monsieur Boudouresques, our bearded mayor. The church wedding took place in our local Eglisette, an 8th century stone chapel.

Fortunately our oldest daughter, Chrish, who was living in Egypt, brought all her help. We had to clean the inside and the outside of this ancient chapel, cutting away brambles, picking up plastic bottles and bags, beer cans, and other unmentionables. Our second daughter Katrin, came all the way from Houston to take charge of the flowers and candles. We managed to hook up an organ to a Volkswagen bus electrical system (there was no electricity). None of the locals could

*Andrea and David, 31 December 1981*

Les Micocouliers cake, left.

court, cypress trees and the vegetable garden. It was truly stupendous!

Another one of her cakes resembled a bed with gorgeous embroidered linen and a Labrador sleeping on it.

For Harry, her nephew, who was in his drum stage, she produced a birthday cake that was a facsimile of a drum kit with chocolate fingers for drum sticks.

Another year she made him a camouflage army tent, complete with soldiers, daggers and rifles.

For my 75th birthday she made a huge Fly Agaric mushroom, with red hat, white dots, gills and stem, simply perfect.

remember any wedding ever having taken place there before.

It was truly beautiful.

Andrea's mother-in-law Belinda managed to get the recipe that was used for the wedding cake for Prince Charles and Lady Diana Spencer, who were married the same year. We gave it to our local pâtissier (the French don't do our kind of wedding cake) and he produced a wonderful masterpiece.

A reception to which all our friends and neighbours were invited took place right after the wedding, and then, at the stroke of midnight, we had a huge feast for family and close friends. We had the traditional New Year's ham and a stuffed turkey, followed by the wedding cake.

That wedding cake must have imprinted itself forcefully in Andrea's head. She developed a talent for making the most amazing cakes for important family occasions.

For my 70th birthday she reproduced, out of a sort of Madeira cake batter and coloured icing, Les Micocouliers, complete with swimming pool, tennis

*75th birthday mushroom cake*

# My Indispensables

All the food writers and all the cook books consider it an anathema to make salad dressing ahead of time. I am not of that school.

### Salad dressing

I guarantee you that my dressing is as good after a week as on the day I make it. Usually I concoct a litre at a time, but when my son J-B or my grandson Nicholas are around, I make 2 litres, and those 2 litres won't last a week. Seriously, I think that they'd eat fried worms as long as there was some of my salad dressing on them! I have rarely had dinner guests who didn't rave about it and ask for the recipe.

The trouble is, some of the ingredients I can only get in Switzerland. When we lived anywhere but in Helvetia, which was most of the time, we would welcome any amount of guests, but they were especially welcome if they brought Cenovis, Thomy mustard and Aromat! Over the years I have managed to find a reasonable substitute for Cenovis, a yeast-based condiment, not too dissimilar to soy sauce. Aromat you can purchase in many places nowadays, though plain kitchen salt is a good substitute and what's more, has no MSG, and any German type mustard will take the place of Swiss Thomy.

What better way to create a healthy, quick

lunch? Assemble some lettuce leaves, two or three radishes, a tomato, a red pepper, half a sliced sweet onion, a handful of steamed green beans, a hard boiled egg, and/or some shavings of Parmesan, maybe a few croûtons, pour 1/3 of a cup of my dressing over it all, et voilà – a great Chef's Salad!

### Peggy's Salad dressing
Mix ½ lb. (220g) of plain yoghurt with 4 tablespoons of German style mustard, add 3 tablespoons of Cenovis or substitute, 3 tablespoons of Aromat (or 2 tablespoons of plain salt), stir until smooth.

Slowly pour in one cup (20 cl) of very good red wine vinegar, stirring constantly. Fill up with olive oil to get 1 litre of dressing altogether. Pour into a glass juice bottle, screw the lid on tight.

Shake vigorously before use.

## My Magic Spice
My friend Sonia once brought me back a little envelope containing a mixture of spices and salt from Australia. I used it for a marinade and liked it a lot.

When I read the list of ingredients, I decided to make something similar.

Over the years I think I have perfected it.

It is scrumptious for enhancing a soup; on a fried egg, on chicken, on sliced tomatoes, in a marinade; you will find umpteen uses for it. It turns a plain slice of fried turkey into a delicacy.

### Peggy's Magic Spice
In an electric coffee mill grind:
3 teaspoons each of black, white, green and red peppercorns
3 dried pieces of porcini or other dried mushrooms
Sprig of dried summer savoury
½ a cup of sea salt
½ bay leaf

## Curried Walnut Oil
This is a very recent addition to my indispensables – and it has now become totally indispensable.

With a little rock salt, it turns a simple boiled potato into a gourmet dish. On sliced tomatoes, on raw fennel, on asparagus, I could go and on. Use it to baste roast chicken, on beet root, on sliced raw mushrooms, on green beans, yes, I am going on and on. Don't forget the salt!

Be sure to take it out of the fridge to reach room temperature before use.

As a bonus, it gives everything a lovely golden colour.

I have a bottle of it on my kitchen counter and use it almost every day, and here is the super simple way to make it:

### Peggy's Curried Walnut Oil
Add two or more teaspoons of your favourite curry powder to a jar of walnut oil, shake, let it stand for 24 hours. Shake before use.

# Boons and Balms

The fields around here furnish so many goodies, they are like an organic herb and spice supermarket.

I collect Roman chamomile in the early summer and dry it. In August I gather wild lavender and wild sage, using one hand for the former and one hand for the latter in order not to mix the aromas.

On other days it's wild fennel seeds and thyme. Sew little sachets using butter muslin or old lace curtains. Fill them with dried fennel, dried sage and dried lavender and add them to your evening bath for a soothing and relaxing effect. The fennel seeds I use in fish marinades and for a stomach-settling tisane.

Summer savoury is just about my favourite herb. I can't imagine green beans without it. Appropriately it is called Bohnenkraut in Switzerland, green bean herb.

Boil the green beans for a few minutes, drain and add them to a saucepan in which you have softened some chopped garlic in butter. Add summer savory and reheat the beans in this mixture. Tisane made from thyme is an excellent substitute for coffee in the morning, especially if you add some chopped ginger to it.

Sage leaves; one of the most effective remedies against a sore throat: chew a fresh sage leaf.

We have four or five old and prolific verveine plants from which I pick literally sack-loads of leaves. I let them dry in the shade then bottle and bag them for all the children and grandchildren to take home from visits. When they infuse the leaves it reminds them of happy lazy days at Les Micocouliers (*below left*).

### Pomegranate Jelly

There are several pomegranate trees at Les Micocouliers (*below right*). They are a very

versatile and adorning addition to the flora. The buds start to appear in March, red first, then bright green.

In June they are in full bloom, and what a bloom, large, orangey-red, spectacular. The fruit doesn't get ripe until November and is at its best in December. The little garnet kernels are delicious, but very messy to extract. I arm myself with a paper towel, go and pick a pomegranate, peel it, bite off a series of kernels and spit out the pips. You can put the kernels in a blender and make lovely pomegranate juice. This is used extensively in Iranian cooking. I also make a few pots of pomegranate jelly

every year. Make juice and proceed as in blackberry jam (page 104). I have just recently read an article extolling the anti-oxidant qualities of pomegranates, another boon!

### Green Weed Soup (*above*)

Use the tough spinach leaves, wild salsify leaves and roots, some dandelions and other weeds of the dandelion family, some sprigs of wild asparagus, wild leeks, 3 or 4 leaves pinched off the broccoli plant and a couple of potatoes for smoothness, boil in chicken broth, put in blender and serve with garlic croûtons and/or a dollop of cream.

## Cardamon Cream Dessert

In my over sixty years of cooking and looking at thousands of recipes I have never come across this delicious dessert, and when I serve it now, everybody says: *oh, yes, very common in the Middle East, old hat.* Well here it is for those who, like me, are not familiar with it.

### Cardamon Cream Dessert

Dissolve 1 cup (220g) of sugar in a mixture of 2 cups (40 cl) of rich yoghurt, 1 cup (20 cl) of whole milk and 1 cup (20 cl) of cream by warming everything to about 120F (45C).
Pound 1 teaspoon of cardamom seeds with a mortar and pestle and add to the cream mixture. Let rest in a cool place overnight.

Next day prepare 6 sheets of gelatin according to the instructions on the package. Stir into the cardamom cream and pass through a fine sieve or some butter muslin.

Pour into one large or 10 small moulds. It will set in about 6 hours.

## Organic Lemons and Oranges

I am very lucky to have a bridge friend, Josephine, who has a green thumb when it comes to growing citrus fruit. She keeps orange and lemon trees in large grape harvest tubs that sit on wooden trolleys. These she can wheel in and out of her garage according to how warm it is. Fortunately she is also very generous and supplies me with her precious crop whenever I need some.

The grated (organic) zest I use for Christmas Mailänderli cookies (page 116) as well as for:

### Moroccan Blood Orange Salad (*below*)

Peel 3 regular and 3 blood oranges, carefully removing as much of the white membrane as possible, but keeping the fruit whole.

With a very sharp knife cut the oranges into slices across the sections. Arrange on a platter, alternating a slice of regular and a slice of red orange. Sprinkle with a bit of cinnamon.

Cut the zest of 2 oranges and 1 lemon into narrow strips and cook them in syrup made with ½ cup (110g) of sugar and a cup of water. Take them out of the pan while still warm and spread over the fruit. A dash of Grand Marnier or Cointreau completes this light dessert.

# Index of recipes